LIST FOR SUCCESS

HOW REAL ESTATE PROFESSIONALS MAKE BIG MONEY

JIM LONDAY

REAL ESTATE EDUCATION COMPANY/CHICAGO
a Longman Group USA Company

While a great deal of care has been taken to provide accurate and current information, the ideas, suggestions, general principles, and conclusions presented in this book are subject to local, state, and federal laws and regulations, court cases, and any revisions of the same. The reader is thus urged to consult legal counsel regarding any points of law—this publication should not be used as a substitute for competent legal advice.

Acquisitions Editor: *Nancy Osman*
Copy Editor: *Carole Bilina*
Cover Design: *Vito DePinto*
Interior Design: *Ophelia Chambliss-Jones*
Manager, Manuscript Production: *Vicki M. Weisberg*

Published by Real Estate Education Company
a subsidiary of Longman Financial Services Publishing, Inc.

Printed in the United States of America.

86 87 88 10 9 8 7 6 5 4 3 2 1

Library of Congress Cataloging-in-Publication Data

Londay, Jim.
  List for success.

  Includes index.
  1. Real estate business. 2. Real estate agents.
I. Title.
HD1375.L66 1986   333.33'068   86–7413
ISBN 0-88462-546-X

**To my loving parents.
Thanks.**

7134668

CONTENTS

PREFACE

This book was written in response to a question I frequently hear from seminar participants: "Where can we find the information you have taught us in book form?" "How to" books on listing residential real estate have been around for a long time but the ideal residential listing book, until now, has not been written. *List For Success* is a step-by-step guide on how to excel in listing residential properties.

The ultimate goal of *List For Success* is to teach you how to increase your income in residential real estate in a professional and ethical manner and to serve as a reference to improve your technique and dialogue as your skills expand. The teaching of specifics, not available in other texts, is stressed.

The book is divided into five sections: Getting Started; Prospecting; Obtaining and Servicing the Listing; Negotiating and Closing the Sale; and Building Referrals and Repeat Business.

Getting Started—Developing objective goals and formulating a plan to achieve them is essential to accomplishing any great task. To this end I have included charts to be used to track production after you have reduced your long-range goals into achievable daily goals. Included is a self-test showing you how much productive time is actually spent with clients in relation to the total time devoted to your profession.

Prospecting—This section explains effective ways to contact more people in less time and how to identify groups of property owners likely to sell in the near future, thus allowing you to make more effective use of your prospecting time. Included are new and innovative direct-mail techniques, fresh approaches to working expired listings and for-sale-by-owners, and a variety of other methods to locate highly motivated sellers.

Prospecting is heavily stressed because listings do not

always go to the most experienced or accomplished salesperson. Most listings go to the *first* salesperson who contacts the prospective seller and presents a professional listing presentation.

The more effective you become at prospecting, the more listings you will obtain and the more income you will earn. It is as simple as that. The suggestions in this portion of the book are designed to make you a super-productive prospector.

Obtaining and Servicing the Listing—Chapters Six and Seven involve educating the seller to the workings of the marketplace and how his or her property can best be marketed. A knowledgeable seller will be more likely to avoid overpricing and market the property so it sells. These chapters discuss the preparation of detailed, aggressive marketing plans designed to produce sales at the top of the fair range of value in the shortest possible time.

Chapter 8 focuses on getting the listing sold after it is on the market. You will learn why a difficult listing is not selling and what remedial marketing steps are needed to make the sale. You will learn to turn complaint calls into constructive action that speeds sales of problem properties.

Negotiating and Closing the Sale—Chapter 9 is geared toward negotiating a sale with the best price and terms for your seller without losing the prospective buyer. You will learn how to "keep the transaction together" when the going gets rocky and the buyer gets shaky.

Chapter 10 teaches you how to close sales smoothly. Special attention is given to closing transactions at the earliest possible date, allowing your sellers to receive their proceeds quickly.

Building Referrals and Repeat Business—"The Future File" teaches you how to capture the loyalty of selling prospects not ready to place their houses on the market. Techniques are taught to ensure that *you* and not another salesperson gets the listings when prospects are ready to sell.

You can ensure long-term success and prosperity by applying the techniques explained in the chapter on building referrals. You will learn who should be in your personal customer file and how to obtain the maximum number of referrals from them. These approaches will allow you to establish yourself as an outstanding professional in your field.

I want to acknowledge the tremendous technical and moral support I received from the following people at Longman Group: Nancy Osman, Manager-Professional Books; Carole Bilina, Senior Copy Editor; and Cheryl Wilson, Development Editor. They deserve much of the credit for the organization and readability of this book. All three get an "A+" for patience. I also want to thank the rest of the support staff at Longman and the reviewers whose comments and suggestions greatly improved the final content. Immeasurable credit is also due the following people: my wife Mary and my three children, Sarah, John, and Bridget; my parents, John and Sophie Londay; and my good friends Ron Hagge and Myrna Powell. My thanks also go out to thousands of students and seminar participants, many of whom contributed ideas and suggestions that eventually became part of the manuscript.

PART I

GETTING STARTED

CHAPTER 1

SETTING OBJECTIVES

This book is a roadmap for you to follow to reach your financial and professional goals in residential real estate sales. It was written with the assumption that you have the desire to become a top-producing professional specializing in listing residential property.

You can more quickly become the success you strive to be by outlining specific objectives and setting a time limit on meeting them. For that reason you need to decide where you want to be before I help you learn how to get there.

DEVELOPING YOUR GOALS

Achievable goals must be specific, objective, measurable, and realistic. Success in realizing goals is accomplished by continually monitoring them and adjusting them to changing conditions. They must be flexible and reflect changes in conditions to remain valid. We will examine how goal-setting can be used to its best advantage.

Have Specific, Measurable Goals

To be effective, goals must be in writing and must be as specific as possible. It is fine to start out with an overall goal of closing $3 million in volume in the coming year but that goal must be broken down into specific components. How much of that volume will come from listings? How much from selling?

You may decide on goals of $1 million from sales and $2 million from listings. The decision of how much volume will come from each should be based partly on your past sales record. For example, if your production for the past year was split 60/40 between listings and sales, you logically could set a goal of closed listing volume of $2 million and closed sales volume of $1 million when planning to reach your overall goal of $3 million in closed volume.

After determining your production goal for the year, break your sales and listing dollar volume goals into unit volume goals. The following is an example of setting a listing goal: Your average sales price on closed listings the past year was $50,000. You will need 40 sold listings in the coming year to obtain your goal of $2 million in closed listing volume. You had a 20 percent expired or cancelled rate for all the listings you obtained last year; you closed transactions on four out of every five listings obtained.

Factoring in that percentage tells you that you will need to obtain 50 listings in the coming year to have 40 of them close and reach the goal of $2 million in closed volume from listing activities. This translates into an easily monitored goal of one listing per week.

In this way break down your yearly production goals into weekly goals. Fifty listings in one year seems like a lot, and it is. This would not be a realistic goal for newer agents. However, many experienced listers exceed this goal year after year.

Your weekly volume goal now needs to be broken down into specific behavioral goals. If you plan to obtain 20 listings from working expired listings, and experience indicates that you obtain one listing for every three days of working expireds, 60 days during the coming year must be devoted to working expireds. An average of five days a month should be devoted to working expireds (*see* Goal-Setting Form, Example 1).

Carry this kind of planning through to the other types of prospecting you plan to use. If you plan to obtain 15 listings from direct mail and your personal program yields one listing for every 300 direct-mail pieces you send out, you should plan to mail 4,500 direct-mail pieces in the coming year. Chapter 2, "Getting Organized," will help you determine how to divide your goals among the different prospecting techniques you use.

Follow through with this exercise until you have specific numbers of activities you must complete to reach your listing

Example 1

GOAL-SETTING FORM
Listings

Step 1. Listing volume goal for the upcoming year: _____
Average price of last year's listings: _____
Divide the yearly goal by last year's
average listing price. This will give
you the total number of listings you
will need to obtain in the upcoming
year: _____

Step 2. Total number of listing presentations completed in the previous year: _____
Total number of listings obtained
last year: _____
Divide the number of listing presentations by the number of listings
obtained. This gives you a ratio: _____

Step 3. Multiply your listing volume goal for
the upcoming year by the ratio obtained in Step 2. This is the number
of presentations you will need to
complete in the upcoming year: _____

Step 4. Divide the number of listing presentations you will need to complete by
52 to determine the number of presentations you will need to com-
plete each week: _____

---

goals for the coming year (*see* Prospecting Summary,
Example 2).

This exercise also must be completed for the selling portion of your goal volume. Specific activities that can be used as
the basis of your goals include the number of open houses you
will need to hold, the number of times per week you will need
to have a prospect in your car, the number of houses you will
need to show per week, the amount of time you will need to

Example 2

PROSPECTING SUMMARY

MONTH OF _____

Expireds

Number of Expireds Contacted

[_____]

Number of Appointments Made   Number of Listings Obtained

[_____] [_____]

For-Sale-by-Owners

Number of FSBOs Contacted

[_____]

Number of Appointments Made   Number of Listings Obtained

[_____] [_____]

Direct Mail

Number of Direct-Mail Respondents Contacted

[_____]

Number of Appointments Made   Number of Listings Obtained

[_____] [_____]

Last Year's Expireds

Number of Last Year's Expireds Contacted

[_____]

Number of Appointments Made   Number of Listings Obtained

[_____] [_____]

Personal Client File Contacts

Number of Personal Clients Contacted

[_____]

Number of Appointments Made   Number of Listings Obtained

[_____] [_____]

---

spend taking duty, and any other activity that has generated sales for you in the past. Include every technique you plan on using to reach your closed sales goal.

Be specific and keep it simple and uncomplicated as you determine exactly what you will have to do to reach your goals. If you know you sell a house every four times you show properties to a valid buying prospect and you also know your average sale is $50,000, you must sell 20 houses to reach your goal of $1 million in sales transactions. This means you will need to conduct 80 showing appointments during the year to reach your goal.

Be Objective

When determining goals, take as much emotion out of the decisions as possible. View your past performance and weigh it against your proposed goals as if they were those of another person. This perspective will allow you to be as realistic as possible in setting goals that are obtainable, yet will require you to stretch your abilities and efforts to the limit.

To reach your full human potential you continually must develop in three areas: family, personal, and business. Setting goals in all three areas is a necessity. Business activities can consume your time unless you schedule time to achieve family and personal goals. Spending adequate time with family and friends helps maintain a positive attitude when on the job.

Develop more goals than you probably will be able to accomplish but make each goal possible and obtainable. Reaching four out of five obtainable goals is far better than not reaching one unobtainable goal. You always can carry over the unattained goals to the next year.

We have discussed breaking down sales volume goals to specific activities. This basis for reaching your overall goal will be valid only if you have set an obtainable overall volume goal. When setting your volume goal, consider all the major factors that will have an effect upon your production. Include the outlook for the local real estate market, projected interest rates, the amount of time you will be devoting to sales, and your past sales record when arriving at a final figure.

If you have been in business for more than two years, you should have a reasonable idea of your capabilities. Set the figure at such an amount that you will have to be at your best for the entire year to reach the goal.

Goal-Setting for New Agents

A new salesperson has no track record on which to base goal-setting. But goal-setting is an undeniable requirement. Being determined to start making money right away is a trait seen in most of the new people who eventually become top producers. Earning your first commission check as quickly as possible is accomplished by setting specific goals the first day of your career and then going to work immediately to make them happen.

What type of goals should you set for yourself? To succeed, you must set both listing and sales goals. A reasonable goal for a new person is to obtain one listing or one sale in the first month in business and do whatever it takes to get it. Goals starting the second month in business should be a minimum of three contracts a month, either listings or sales, preferably two listings and one sale.

Too many new people only sell and do not list. Disaster! You must list if you want to last. Why do new people sell rather than list? Because selling requires different skills than listing. Also, the competition for buyers is less than that for sellers.

Buyers Buy Houses, Sellers Buy Agents

Different skills are used to sell a house to a qualified buyer than the skills necessary to list the house of a knowledgeable seller. Relatively unskilled salespersons often are successful with buyers if they have the time, patience, and persistence required to persevere with a buyer until they find a house the buyer falls in love with. Sellers must be convinced that you are the person best qualified to quickly sell their house for the largest amount of money possible. Working with sellers generally requires more technique than is needed when working with the majority of buyers. This book was written specifically to teach this technique.

Start your career by concentrating on prospecting for and obtaining listings whenever you do not have a qualified, motivated buyer with whom to work. Ensure long-term success by learning to become a good lister at the beginning of your career.

Goal-Setting Summary

Setting goals is as much an art as it is a science. Start by setting all your "need to" goals such as income and sales volume targets. Work your way to your "like to" goals such as obtaining an appraiser's license or earning a Certified Residential Specialist designation.

Make a written record of all your goals. Be as specific as possible and break down each general goal to the smallest identifiable behavior that will help you reach that goal. Be objective when deciding how high to set each goal. Make each goal difficult but possible to reach. Do not be afraid to dream a little. Set some goals that seem out of reach at the present but are obtainable in the long run through planning and hard work.

OBTAINING YOUR GOALS

A person can use two valuable approaches to help reach his or her goals. One is to take ten minutes each day and plan what he or she will do that day to stay on track in reaching his or her goals (*see* Daily Planning Sheet, Example 3). This takes only minutes yet gives you a specific plan for the day and works effectively to minimize procrastination. Many people find it to be most effective when done at the end of each workday, enabling them to wake up the next day with a specific plan of action. When filling out your Daily Planning Sheet, keep in mind not only the urgency but the importance of each task you place on your list. Concentrate on completing the tasks that will best help you reach your overall stated goals.

The following technique is the best way I have found of reminding a person on a daily basis how he or she is progressing toward his or her stated yearly goals: Draw three large graphs with your listing, sales, and closed volume goals for the year broken down in weekly increments (*see* Examples 4, 5, and 6). Along the bottom horizontal line of each graph, identify a column for each Saturday in the year. The vertical column will consist of your volume goal.

You must place these charts where you and other people will see them every day, preferably in your office where your colleagues and sales manager will be aware of them. You are thus telling the world what your goals are. This is a tremendous motivator.

Last, in your appointment book make a notation at the end of every three-month period to review each of your goals. On those dates, it will be time to modify your goals.

Example 3

DAILY PLANNING SHEET

To Be Done Today   Phone Calls
(Number in order of
importance)
_____   _____

_____   _____

_____   _____

_____   _____

_____   _____

_____   _____

_____   _____

_____   _____

_____   _____

_____

Thoughts and Ideas   Correspondence and
                                      Thank-You Notes
_____   _____

_____   _____

_____   _____

_____   _____

_____   _____

_____   _____

_____   _____

_____   _____

_____   _____

Example 4

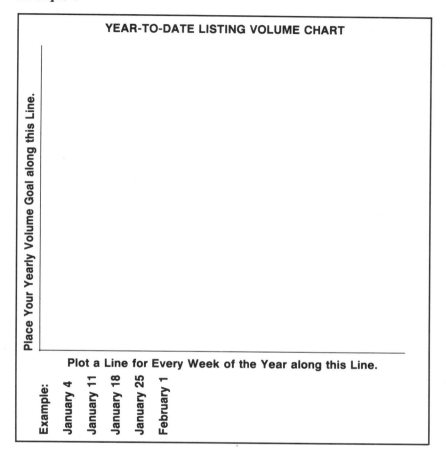

Modify Your Goals

Modify goals? What am I talking about? When people make goals, they should go for them until they get them! The "old college try" attitude is counterproductive when working toward long-term goals.

A set of goals is relevant only when it is obtainable and challenging. Circumstances change. On January 1, we have no idea what our personal or business situations will be October 1. Because we do not know what the future holds, we have to adjust our goals to keep them fresh and meaningful.

Example 5

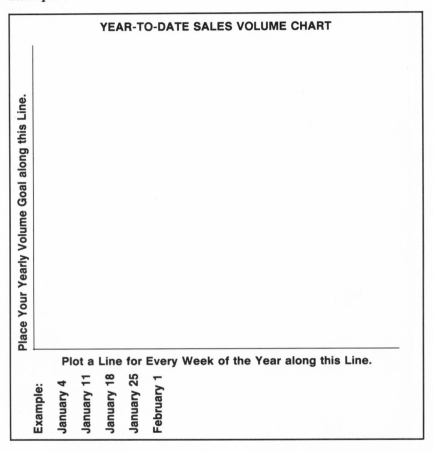

Suppose you become acquainted with a builder and he or she lists 15 houses with you on September 1. You have had a good year up to that point and those 15 listings push you over your listing goal for the entire year. Are you going to quit looking for listings because you reached your goal? Of course not! That is why we adjust.

If you must lower your sights to keep your goals achievable, do it. That is the only way the goals will continue to mean anything. If we do not adjust goals to keep them challenging and obtainable, they cease to serve their purpose.

The purpose of goal-setting and monitoring is to keep you

Example 6

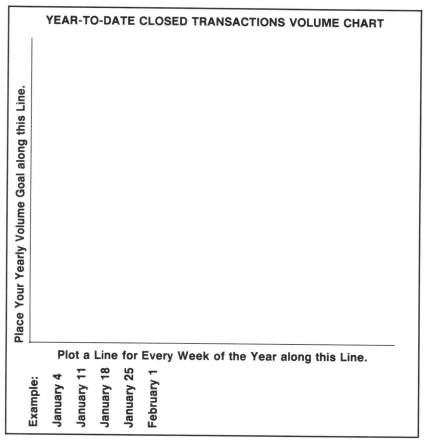

focused on what is important and motivate you to be the best you can be. Use goals as a tool, not as a rigid set of rules that confine and restrict the way you approach life and business.

STAYING MOTIVATED

With motivation, a person has enthusiasm. With enthusiasm, you will win. It is that simple. The more enthusiasm you have, the more business you will do; the more business you do, the more enthused you become . . . and on . . . and on . . . and on. A person riding a crest of success can be incredibly productive for long stretches of time. The following are some techniques you can use to keep your motivation high.

Professionals who vary the ways in which they prospect for business take an active part in keeping themselves fresh. For example, after working for-sale-by-owners for three weeks, you may be ready for a fresh challenge and switch to working expireds for a while. After calling on expireds for a few weeks, you may want to spend your prospecting time calling on former buyers to get some referral business. Keep your enthusiasm high by periodically starting a new listing campaign using different prospecting approaches. Keep fresh by changing approaches and continually trying new things.

Surround yourself with successful people. Work in an office of very high producers. Working among and with high-volume, established professionals is a great motivator.

You will receive many benefits from spending time with successful people. Surrounding yourself with winners is a great learning experience. They are in a position to give you valuable advice and guidance because of the wealth of experience they have in listing properties and putting sales together. Associating with first-class people heightens your self-image and increases your skills. Associating with the cream of the crop of our profession is also personally rewarding. The nicest and best people in the real estate business in most cases are the top-producing people. That is how they got where they are.

Develop the habit of using books and tapes to keep yourself fresh. Do not limit yourself to real estate–related material. Some of the best ideas, inspirations, and innovative approaches in real estate have come from studying material used in other professions. Keep an open mind. Approach problems from a fresh, new outlook.

A real estate agent with a winning attitude exhibits many qualities: a results-oriented approach to problems, a positive outlook, and a knack for cooperating with people. Many of these attributes are often present in highly successful agents. But the trait most common to top-producing people is that they approach business and life aggressively. Being assertive is a great asset. Lead, follow, or get out of the way!

CHAPTER 2

GETTING ORGANIZED

This chapter is a collection of ideas and techniques designed to help you get more done in less time.

SOURCE-OF-BUSINESS REVIEW

This exercise should be completed at the end of each calendar year but it can be profitably put into effect at any time. The first step is to complete the three Production Tally Forms. They are the Listing Tally Sheet, Sales Tally Sheet, and Closed Volume Tally Sheet (Examples 7, 8, and 9).

Completing these forms will give you a total log of listings, sales, and closed transactions and will enable you to determine the sources of your business. The most important entry is the source or prospecting technique used to generate the original prospect of each transaction. You can then direct your efforts to the activities that are most productive for you.

The next step is to determine how much business you closed from each source or prospecting technique. For this, transfer the information from your log to the Source-of-Business Summary Form (Example 10). It has columns for the most common sources from which real estate people obtain leads. They include: referrals, direct mail, working expireds, working for-sale-by-owners (FSBOs), holding open houses, and taking duty time. There are also blank columns you can use for other categories. I prefer logging dollar volume but you may use either dollar volume or number of transactions for each category.

Example 7

LISTING TALLY SHEET				
DATE	ADDRESS	SOURCE	LISTING PRICE	YEAR-TO-DATE

Example 8

SALES TALLY SHEET				
DATE	ADDRESS	SOURCE	SALES PRICE	YEAR-TO-DATE

Example 9

CLOSED VOLUME TALLY SHEET				
DATE	ADDRESS	SOURCE	SALES PRICE	YEAR-TO-DATE

Example 10

SOURCE-OF-BUSINESS SUMMARY

ADDRESS	REFERRAL	EXPIREDS	FSBO	DIRECT MAIL	OPEN HOUSE	DUTY TIME	—	—	

When you have transferred the information, total each column. You will then know how much of your business was generated from each of the sources and techniques on which you work and rely. The Source-of-Business Summary will show you which approaches are most effective for you and will help you decide where to devote the major thrust of your efforts in the coming year.

If you spent equal amounts of time working FSBOs and expireds and obtained twice as many listings from expireds as you did from FSBOs, you will know that you could work expireds more and spend less time with FSBOs. If you have spent a lot of time on expireds but have gotten very little business from them, you should either drop expireds or learn to work them better.

Spending 30 minutes completing this easy exercise is an eye-opener. I have yet to have a person do this who was not surprised at how the figures came out. For example, a woman in her third year in the business attended one of my seminars. After the seminar, she told me that her first two years in the business had been good, but that her production had fallen off considerably in her third year. I suggested she complete a Source-of-Business Summary. She did and learned that a large proportion of her business in her first two years had come from manning open houses. At the beginning of her third year she started avoiding open houses because she incorrectly thought they were unproductive for her. She started manning opens again and her production jumped immediately.

You can learn a lot from this exercise. It will tell you if you are obtaining the amount of referral business you should for the time you have been in business. If a person has been in business more than two years, a red flag should pop up in front of his or her eyes if less than one-half of the volume is from referrals. The person had better do some research and find out what he or she is doing wrong. Most likely, it is a failure to stay in touch with former customers (*see* Chapter 12, "Developing a Loyal Clientele").

Many people find duty time an effective way to prospect. They have mastered phone techniques to the point where they are unusually effective when handling ad and sign calls. They have learned how to "get the name" and "get the appointment." Other people find that duty time provides the least amount of business of all prospecting approaches for time and effort expended. If you find duty time unprofitable, see if you can arrange with your manager to quit taking duty time or have another person who finds duty time productive sit in for you. You can then devote that time to prospecting techniques more suitable to you. You will soon be one of the top-producing agents in your company. If duty time is ineffective for you, it is self-defeating to wait until your sales volume is high before quitting duty time.

The next step is to fill out the Waste-Cutter Review (Example 11). Obtain the information needed by analyzing the entries in your appointment book for the previous week. Make copies of this form and work backward week-by-week through your appointment book until a pattern emerges. The purpose is to pinpoint nonproductive activities that routinely use up your valuable time. Make short notes on any regularly occurring activities that did not involve being with prospects.

Critically analyze every activity. The first year I did this I was amazed at the amount of time wasted on activities that had become rituals yet provided no income-producing results. Many of the routine activities a person goes through daily can seem important. Frequently they are. But when they become a substitute for being with prospects, priorities have been misplaced and it is time for some of them to be eliminated or done less frequently. **An agent's first priority must be spending time with customers: prospecting, listing, selling, and closing.**

Do not misunderstand me; activities like attending sales meetings and going on tour are important. But if you have a perfect attendance record for meetings and tours and a substandard sales record, you could be spending too much time "getting ready" to see prospects and not enough time actually working with them.

Your first Source-of-Business Summary will reveal a basis for numerous changes you could make in how you use your time. Every year you do this summary, there will be fewer and less dramatic changes. After three years you will find yourself making mostly minor fine-tuning adjustments.

You will be getting up in the morning to get dressed and earn money instead of getting dressed to go to the office hoping something will happen that will result in a commission.

Example 11

THE WASTE-CUTTER REVIEW		
Servicing Current Business		

Time Spent

Servicing Listings		
Servicing Pendings		
Attending Closings		

Prospecting

Contacting Past Clients		
Working Expireds		
Working FSBOs		
Direct Mail		
Other		
Other		

Working With Current Prospects

Obtaining Listings		
Prospect Follow-up		
Working with Buyers		

Other

Duty Time		
Open Houses		
New Listing Tour		
Sales Meetings		
Classes/Seminars		
Paperwork		
Other		
Other		

THE ONE-YEAR TEST

After completing the Waste-Cutter Review, conduct the One-Year Test. This consists of completely going through your offices at work and at home. Include everything: file cabinets, desk drawers, bookcases. Everything!

Follow one hard-and-fast rule. If you have not used it or needed it in the last year, throw it away. The only exceptions are the files you will store indefinitely: closed sales, completed appraisals, files that are rarely used, and your personal real estate library of sales tapes, books, and periodicals. Store these in a place separate from your normal work area.

The first time I conducted my One-Year Test, I filled eight large garbage bags with worthless materials. Now I throw out only one small bag a year. Before I started throwing things away, I was buried in stacks of files, old multiple-listing books, ads, periodicals, and papers. I was spending more time looking for files than working on them.

After 14 years of selling real estate, my real estate brokerage business was contained in two file drawers and one desk drawer. These drawers included Rolodexes containing my personal customer list, currently active files, Future Files (*see* Chapter 11), listing presentation materials, forms, and directories. What more do you need to sell real estate? Nothing. Get rid of the rest. Increase your efficiency by cleaning house with a vengeance.

I HAVE REALLY BEEN WORKING

You probably think you have . . . but, if you want to find out, do this interesting exercise. Keep accurate track of the time you actually spend with prospects. The only time you can count is when you are face-to-face with prospects or talking to them on the telephone. This enlightening self-test is easily done. All you do is carry the "I Have Really Been Working" Tally Sheet with you (Example 12) and write down the amount of time spent with buyers and sellers. In a week or two you will realize how little time you spend prospecting, listing, selling, or closing.

How many times have you gone home and said to your spouse, "Boy, did I put in a long day today. Ten hours! You sure need stamina to be in the real estate business!"? Ten hours does

Example 12

DATE	NAME OF PROSPECT OR LISTING	ACTIVITY (showing houses, open house, listing presentation, etc.)	BEGIN-NING TIME	END-ING TIME	ELAPSED TIME
					TOTAL

"I HAVE REALLY BEEN WORKING" TALLY SHEET

not sound so impressive when you realize that you spent five hours in the office, one and one-half hours at lunch, 45 minutes on breaks, two hours on duty, one and one-half hours in the car running errands, and 15 minutes showing a house to a prospect.

If you have never been guilty of this, my comments do not count. But if you have, take a small measure of comfort in the fact that I am also pointing a finger at myself. The point is that many people often spend far less time seeing prospects than they think they do. This exercise is easy to complete and will tell you how effectively you spend your working day.

GETTING THE WORK DONE

A successful real estate person's time should be spent with prospective buyers and sellers. However, there is plenty of paperwork that needs to be done, especially if this business is approached correctly: mailing newsletters, using direct mail, and preparing two or three listing presentations every week (*see* Chapters 3, 7, and 12). Fortunately, there are some practical solutions to this problem.

Personal Secretary

Once established in the business, many successful people find a personal secretary indispensable as well as cost-effective. If a salesperson is properly organized, a part-time secretary working an average of five to 15 hours a week will allow him or her to spend more time making money and less time doing clerical work. Hiring a part-time secretary is not feasible for most new people but should be strongly considered when you get to the point where you have a problem scheduling sufficient time to service your customers' needs.

What should your secretary do? He or she should handle every aspect of your direct-mail programs. After your secretary is trained, except for giving him or her specific instructions, a person should not have to devote any time to direct mail. A secretary can also update customer files, file sold comps, obtain information from loan companies and the courthouse, and type listing agreements, seller's estimated net sheets, and correspondence.

Effective use of a secretary can reduce the time you spend running errands. Going to the office supply store, delivering contracts, picking up printing, and putting up signs use valuable time and should be done by someone else whenever possible. Use your secretary for simple tasks that will free your time for prospects. The office secretary in your sales office will not have time to do these things for you. In most cases, getting them done is your responsibility. Check with your sales manager to determine the specific duties of your office secretary and what assistance he or she is allowed to provide individual persons.

Sources

There are a number of sources for locating good part-time secretaries. One of the best is a local college or university that offers a real estate major. Contact the head of the real estate department and tell him or her your specific needs. In most cases, he or she will provide you with a list of students who are anxious to work. Hiring college students who are majoring in real estate benefits everyone. You will have an employee who has an interest in what you are doing and for that reason will probably be conscientious. The student benefits by getting exposure and practical experience in the field he or she plans to enter.

Another good source for part-time secretarial help is local high schools. Most high schools have programs that match prospective employers with students. One advantage is the likelihood of hiring a secretary who lives close to your home or office, thus eliminating the long commute that can be a problem when an employee works only a few hours a day.

One often overlooked source of part-time help is local job-placement agencies for retired persons. With luck, you will find a person with a wealth of office experience, thus cutting down the time needed to train your new employee. Many retired secretaries need little or no direction and can even help you streamline your office procedures.

Secretarial Service

Using a professional secretarial service is another way to reduce the amount of time spent on paperwork. For many functions a secretarial service is superior to having your own secretary because a service normally has word-processing equipment capable of storing mailing lists. This equipment saves time and money.

Your newsletter mailing list, "listing farm" mail lists, or lists used repeatedly for specific direct-mail programs easily can be updated, once entered into the system. Any time you need to put out a mailing, the entire list can be printed directly on plain labels.

Secretarial services are also the best option when a person has large volumes of typing. The prices are competitive with having your own secretary, plus your office or typewriter is not tied up.

Keeping Records

Established real estate people need to have a system to keep track of customers and to remind a person to follow up and contact prospects on specific future dates. Simplicity is the key to making any system work. Some people need only a few packs of index cards, some file folders, and an appointment book to satisfactorily keep track of things.

There are a variety of index card systems, personal computer systems, and file folder systems that different people use. No one system is right for everyone. You must decide on a system, implement it, and improve its effectiveness while using it. Keep it simple. Record and keep the information in the briefest form possible. Picture yourself as a real estate professional who spends the majority of his or her time with prospects. Do not attempt bookkeeping as an avocation.

ADVICE FOR NEW AGENTS

New people should not say anything, do anything, or have anything printed that would indicate that they are new to the business. Buying and selling prospects want to work with experienced people. Increase your chances for obtaining business by projecting the image of a trained professional. Do not be dishonest. Just avoid advertising the fact that you have limited experience.

Every new person has a few embarrassing moments. I did when I was new and you will, too. Do not let these situations bother you. They will pass and you soon will be able to laugh about them. But do not embarrass yourself or lose potential business by broadcasting the fact that you are new in the business.

Courses, seminars, training sessions, books, and tapes have their place and make valuable contributions in orienting a new person to the nature of real estate sales. But they are no substitute for working with real buyers and sellers. Take every available chance to see a customer even if he or she is not an excellent prospect. Practicing on the tire-kickers when your schedule permits is better than role-playing. You then will be better equipped to handle situations of true prospects with immediate needs.

One excellent way for newly licensed people to get a lot of experience fast is to actively work expired listings (Chapter 4) or FSBOs (Chapter 5). Working expireds hard every day during the first six weeks of your real estate career will cram what is normally one year's worth of talking to actual sellers into one and one-half months.

By taking duty time and sitting at open houses, the typical novice might see an average of two or three lukewarm prospects in one week. By actively working expireds or FSBOs, a new person can talk to ten, 15, or even 20 honest prospects every day. This aggressive initial approach produces people who last in the business and prosper.

In their initial months in the business, many people are reluctant to ask for help. They will work half a dozen FSBOs and stumble and fail at the same point in every attempt. The person will think that FSBOs are not for him or her and will try something else instead of identifying and correcting the errors in the approach.

When in need of assistance, look for and accept help. Who should you look to for advice? Your sales manager is the logical choice and is usually a good source of information. Do not rely solely on your manager, however, or you will miss out on a wealth of effective approaches and techniques being used by the "pros" in your office. The best way to learn is to absorb the knowledge of the successful people in real estate sales you want to emulate. Many professionals in this business are willing to share their knowledge with less experienced salespeople. Their extensive experience gives them a vast resource of practical knowledge. When it is shared with someone new, it provides a basis for accelerated learning.

When you talk to experienced people, concentrate on retaining the "how to" material. Take what you learn and try it out in the field. Critique how it worked and adapt it so it is most effective for you. By continually trying new things and being flexible, you can increase your chances of succeeding and prospering in real estate sales.

PROMOTING HEALTHY OFFICE RELATIONSHIPS

A winning attitude produces great results and turns people into top producers. Top-producing people spend most of their time with prospects. They generally do not have time to socialize at the office, and the volume of business they conduct frequently requires them to be absent from sales meetings and tours.

To maintain optimum working relationships with fellow agents, top producers make their best efforts to attend the most important professional and social functions held by the company, while keeping business obligations and opportunities their first priority. Reserve the office for work only. Socialize away from the office.

Develop healthy working relationships with the people in your office. Treat your colleagues with respect. Do not knock the competition. This rule also applies to the people in your office. Gossip and rumors can fly thick and fast in a real estate sales office. Do not participate. People who are highly respected and easiest to work with never speak in a negative way about their fellow workers. Be a professional and you will be treated like one.

PART II
PROSPECTING

CHAPTER 3

DIRECT-MAIL PROSPECTING

Direct mail is the new wave in residential real estate prospecting. Aggressive salespersons and companies that know how to use it are reaping enormous benefits in increased sales volume. By reducing prospecting time and providing high-quality prospects, direct mail allows a salesperson to spend more of his or her time face to face with buyers and sellers—where you need to be if you are to succeed.

We will examine three direct-mail programs designed to find motivated selling prospects in a cost-effective way.

THE OPEN HOUSE/JUST LISTED!/JUST SOLD! PROGRAM

This program services and promotes current listings while providing a continuous supply of listing leads through a mailing of 200 or more promotional brochures in the immediate vicinity of a current listing. Included is a business reply card offering a no-cost, no-obligation market analysis. The two pieces are mailed in a standard #10 envelope. A cover letter is optional but not necessary if the business reply card is correctly designed.

Selecting the Mailing List

Brochures are mailed to homeowners in the area immediately surrounding the listing you are promoting. If the house is located in a clearly defined subdivision, start there. If the subdivision does not have enough houses for a complete mailing, expand into the next area. Every house on the same street as the listing should receive a brochure. Word will spread quickly and positive feedback will soon find its way to your seller.

At times a listing is located between a higher-priced neighborhood and one that is less expensive. In this instance direct your mail to the higher-priced area. It costs the same to sow each seed, so plant it in the most fertile ground available.

Obtain names and addresses from the most recent reverse directory. A reverse directory lists residents by street and address number and makes the compilation of a neighborhood mailing list easy. Address mailers with the addressee's name rather than labeling the envelopes "homeowner" or "resident" if the expense is not too great.

Determining the Desirability of an Area

Before using any direct-mail program, be sure there is enough market activity in an area to justify the effort and expense. Direct mail works but only when mailed to neighborhoods with a high rate of sales turnover.

Subdivisions less than five years old are prime direct-mail targets. Resale activity is at its highest during the first five years of a subdivision's existence. You are competing against the builder but the properties you are listing have the advantages of established landscaping, drapes, wallpaper, and other added amenities the new homes will not offer. Many times, based on whether interest rates are going up or down, the existing homes you will list will also have attractive financing that can be assumed or wrapped by potential buyers. Plus, in most cases the builder has steadily been raising prices, thereby bringing up the value of houses previously built in the subdivision. All these factors make new subdivisions excellent targets for direct-mail campaigns.

Another area that produces good results is a starter neighborhood, an area in which young couples buy their first house. These couples frequently sell this first house within four or five years as their families and income grow and they move into a more expensive and exclusive neighborhood. Starter areas are prime prospecting targets because of this relatively rapid resale time.

Neighborhoods that are changing in character are also well suited to direct-mail prospecting. Most salespersons ignore these areas because they no longer are attractive to some buyers. Just because an area is not the most desirable in the city does not mean you should rule it out as an area in which to prospect. These are great direct-mail areas for two reasons: There is heavy turnover and real estate salespersons rarely work them. You will encounter very little competition for a large pool of potential listings.

Some of the most desirable areas to buyers are the least profitable to prospect, no matter what type of prospecting method you use, because they have very little turnover. In addition, the competition for listings in these areas is usually intense. There is more competition for less business in the most desirable areas in a city, whereas the areas with the highest turnover rates are the areas least worked by real estate salespersons. You generally will find that the more exclusive an area is, the less productive it will be to prospect. Another type of area that produces limited success when using direct-mail prospecting is established neighborhoods. These are often 20 to 30 years old with a firmly entrenched group of resident homeowners. The amount of resales is usually not high enough to provide worthwhile results.

To determine the market activity in any area you are considering for a prospecting project, use the multiple-listing service (MLS) computer or "sold" records to determine how many sales have been closed in the last six to nine months. Areas with a high percentage of recent sales are the most desirable in which to prospect. Expenditures of time and money in direct-mail prospecting are best rewarded when you have researched the recent sales activity in your target area. **Direct mail works, but only if mailed to areas with a high rate of turnover.**

Preparing the Brochure

A competent secretary can prepare a camera-ready brochure in a very short time. A black and white, instant photograph provides acceptable results. Some agents have a screen print made from the photograph. Depending on the reproduction process, this may or may not be necessary.

The address, open house date, and open house time should be a prominent part of the brochure. There are three easy approaches to achieve a professional or typeset look. The first is to use prepared lettering strips that are commercially available through Kroy, 3M, and other companies. The second option is press-on lettering. It comes in a variety of sizes and styles and is available at office supply stores. The cost is nominal. It is somewhat tedious to use, but if carefully applied, produces nice results (*see* Examples 13, 14, and 15). The third approach is to use an electronic typewriter that types in bold print. Results are excellent, it takes little effort, and there is virtually no cost. The main disadvantage is that you are limited in the size of type. A large variety of type styles are usually available.

The text of the brochure can be prepared on any good office typewriter with a fresh ribbon. Type your brochure on your standard company letterhead. Postal regulations require a return address somewhere in your mailer if you use bulk mail rates. If you do not want a return address on the envelope, put it on your brochure.

Reproduction

The latest generation of office copiers produces a high-quality brochure at a very reasonable cost. Access to a good copier makes the application of this program quick and easy. If you have the equipment and keep it simple, you can put out an entire mailing in a few hours. If your office does not have a suitable copier, take the master copy of your brochure to a printer. Many "quick print" shops now have high-volume copiers in addition to offset presses. Normally you can have your brochures copied while you wait. This makes implementing the program fairly easy even if your office does not have a quality copier.

Your mailer provides prospects with their first impression of you. Take care to create an attractive brochure. Be sure that the spelling, punctuation, and grammar are correct. Do your best with the available tools to produce a good-looking brochure, but do not let an obsession with perfection keep you from getting the mail out. Note: When mailing "Just Sold" brochures, omit any reference to the price the property sold for.

The Cover Letter and Business Reply Card

One of the objectives of this program is to promote the property or properties you currently have for sale. The brochure should

Example 13

OPEN HOUSE BROCHURE

OPEN
SUNDAY
1:00 - 3:00

14622 Division

Great loan assumption with possible seller carryback on the immacu-late six-year-old split entry. Large country kitchen fully equipped with self-cleaning range/oven, dishwasher, and disposal. Full wall brick fireplace in the lower-level family room. Large deck. Chain link–fenced rear yard. Walking distance to public and parochial grade and high schools. Location! Condition! Financing! It's got it all! For additional information or to arrange a private showing, call Jim Londay at 555-2380 or 555-5443.

Example 14

JUST SOLD! BROCHURE

WE JUST SOLD YOUR NEIGHBOR'S HOUSE IN

1   2   3   4   5
6   7   8   9   10

DAYS!!

We've just sold your neighbor's house located at 2625 Radcliffe Drive and are looking for additional properties to sell in your area. If you are thinking of selling or merely want to know what your house is worth, please contact me. I'll prepare a market analysis that will tell you the approximate value of your property and what you would net from a sale at that price. There is no cost or obligation for this service. If interested, please call me or fill in the enclosed card and drop it in the mail. No postage is necessary. Thanks for your time.

Jeanette Murphy
555-2380
555-8042

Example 15

JUST LISTED! BROCHURE

JUST LISTED!!

911 Belle Plaine
Unique ranch plan featuring four bedrooms and a "captain's nook" loft that may be used as a playroom or fifth bedroom. 14' x 26' living room features skylights, an energy-saving fireplace, and glass doors leading to a large shaded deck. A perfect house for entertaining with a 15' x 38' walk-out family room with an adjacent kitchenette. The kids will be able to keep themselves occupied for hours. Six-foot cedar privacy fence surrounds the spacious side and back yards. All this plus a low-interest, assumable FHA loan. Call Jim Londay: 555-2380 or 555-5443.

provide the potential buying prospect with all pertinent information regarding the subject property. The second objective is to obtain additional seller and buyer leads if the recipients are not interested in the subject property. A well-constructed business reply card explains what you have to offer a prospective buyer or seller and eliminates the need for a separate cover letter. After sending out thousands of pieces of mail, I found that the inclusion of a cover letter made no significant difference in the amount of business generated, as long as I included a well-designed business reply card.

The business reply card is the most important piece of your mailer because it offers your services and makes it easy for a prospect to contact you. Merely including a reply card increases the amount of business derived from direct-mail prospecting approximately two to three times. Your reply card should: (1) convey an image of professionalism, (2) develop interest, (3) offer your services, and (4) make it easy for a prospect to contact you.

1. Convey professionalism—This is accomplished by using high-quality card stock, professional typesetting, and intelligent copy. Use a conservative layout and type styles. Your typesetter can help you with this. You want to convey the impression of being established and experienced. This is a real plus for less-experienced salespersons because it gives the recipient the impression that you are a successful professional in your field.

2. Develop interest—If you use a two-piece, fold-over format, you can devote the entire front cover to drawing the prospect's attention. Relate the copy to your prospect's interests. Tie it to his or her home, neighborhood, situation, or needs. A simple, but effective lead-in could read: "YOUR HOME . . . probably the best investment you ever made, but . . . do you know its value today?" (*see* Example 17).

3. Inform the prospect of what you have to offer—In the fold-over format, the inside front cover is best used to promote yourself and your company. It should have: (a) your company logo, (b) your offer of assistance to buyers and sellers, (c) your name and phone numbers, and (d) your photo. These items are printed on the inside cover for a very good reason: When people fill out and return the bottom portion of the mailer, they are

Example 16

FOLD-OVER FORMAT BROCHURE   Side One

LONDAY
REAL ESTATE COMPANY

I'll provide an estimate of its fair market value
at no cost or obligation to you. Please call me or fill
in the attached card and drop it in the mail.
No postage is necessary.

Thanks very much

Jim Londay

Jim Londay
Associate Broker

JIM LONDAY
OFFICE: 339–2380
RES: 733–5443

NO POSTAGE IS NECESSARY

☐ I AM INTERESTED IN A NO OBLIGATION ESTIMATE OF
   THE MARKET VALUE OF MY PROPERTY.

☐ I AM INTERESTED IN BUYING A HOME. LOCATED IN
   (CITY/STATE) _____

Name _____ Phone _____

Address _____

City _____ State _____ Zip _____

R
REALTOR®

IF NOT INTERESTED AT THIS TIME PLEASE KEEP THIS CARD
IT IS GOOD INDEFINITELY

MULTIPLE LISTING SERVICE
MLS

Example 17

FOLD-OVER FORMAT BROCHURE   Side Two

OMAHA, NE. 68157
5001 EDINBURGH
JAMES K. LONDAY

POSTAGE WILL BE PAID BY·

FIRST CLASS PERMIT NO. 4876 OMAHA, NE
BUSINESS REPLY MAIL

NO POSTAGE
NECESSARY
IF MAILED
IN THE
UNITED STATES

Your Home . . .
Probably the Best
Investment You Ever Made
But
Do You Know It's Value Today?

left with the top part, which then becomes an oversized business card.

The actual offer of your services is also on the upper inside portion of the card. Keep this short, no more than three or four sentences. Suggested phrasing: "I'll provide an estimate of your property's fair market value at no cost or obligation to you. Please call me, or fill in the attached card and drop it in the mail. No postage is necessary," signed (salesperson's signature with name and title underneath) (*see* Examples 16 and 17).

Stress the words "no cost or obligation" in your advertising and when talking to prospective customers. In our business, our services are all no cost and no obligation until a listing or purchase agreement is signed. Use this fact to your advantage to take away the natural reluctance many people have when thinking of listing or selling a house.

The bottom half of the fold-over card is the actual business reply card containing the information section to be filled out by the prospect. Offer two options to your prospects. The first should be the offer of a no-cost, no-obligation market analysis of their property. The second is to be checked if the person is interested in purchasing a home. Provide indicated blanks for the prospect's name, complete address, and phone numbers. The following statement can be included in small type at the bottom of the card: "If not interested at this time, please keep this card. It is good indefinitely." Many of these cards are kept by people who anticipate moving sometime in the near future. Prospects often call or return cards more than a year after receiving them. The inclusion of this sentence frequently will get a "Future File" prospect to file your card with his or her real estate papers (*see* Chapter 11). The reverse side of the bottom portion of the card has the post office business reply symbol, your reply permit number, and the address to which the card is to be mailed (your home or office).

4. Make it easy for a prospect to contact you—Designed as described, the fold-over reply card gives the prospect the option of calling or filling in the card and dropping it in the mail. Many people are afraid to pick up a phone and call a person providing a professional service. This is true in the case of doctors, lawyers, insurance agents, and, yes, real estate salespersons. By adding a mail-in option and eliminating the necessity of making a phone call, a reply card produces responses from people who would otherwise not contact you. Many salespersons find it productive to include a business reply card in every outgoing piece of local mail. This offers your services to dozens of potential prospects over a period of a year who would otherwise not be contacted.

The Envelope

The contents for this type of mailing fit easily in a standard #10 business envelope. Many agencies prefer that you use their company logo in the return address space. A second, and better, option is to use a line drawing of a pleasant residential scene.

Another possibility when mailing to a specific neighborhood or subdivision is to have "I love (name of subdivision)" printed in the return address space of the envelope. People are interested in news about their neighborhood. This slogan attracts extra attention and provides additional impetus for the homeowner to open the envelope. You can save time and avoid the mess of using bulk rate stamps by having your bulk rate permit number printed on the envelope. As with every part of your mailer, keep the envelope simple.

Prospective Buyers

Buying prospects more frequently call rather than use the business reply card. Their needs are usually more immediate than those of prospective sellers. In most instances they are interested in immediate information on the property you have advertised. If at all possible, make an appointment to show the house to them. You will be reaping one of the main benefits of this program—a buying prospect for your listing. I sold one of every 15 properties advertised in this way. At the very least, you will get a showing and obtain valuable feedback that can aid you and your seller. If the caller determines the listed house does not meet his or her other needs, make an appointment to work with him or her to find what he or she is looking for, possibly another of your company's listings.

Prospective Sellers

In the majority of cases, prospective sellers will use the reply card rather than calling. I have found it to be true in approximately three-fourths of the replies from listing prospects. Potential listers who call rather than use the reply card are usually at the point where they are ready to list at the present time and deserve your immediate and full attention. There are exceptions to the above patterns, but for the most part, they prevail.

A listing prospect who calls will usually refer to receiving your mailer and indicate his or her interest in having a no-cost, no-obligation market analysis completed on his or her house. You will be surprised at the large number who will refer to the "no cost, no obligation" phrase on the business reply card. Do not let this deter you. Most of the people who "make sure" there is no obligation are using that as a last line of defense before admitting to themselves that they need professional help.

Your purpose when receiving one of these calls is to make an appointment. I suggest a short introduction such as the following:

"Thanks very much for your call, Mrs. Smith. I'll be pleased to prepare a market analysis on your house. This normally takes two visits. The first will take only 20 to 30 minutes in which I will measure your house and obtain information necessary to prepare my market analysis. After I've done my research, I'll meet with you to share my conclusions and explain how I arrived at them."

Give the prospect a choice of times when setting up the initial appointment:

"Would two this afternoon or seven this evening be preferable?"

This frequently is referred to as an "alternative of choice."

A different approach is used with a listing prospect who makes use of the reply card. You will initiate the phone conversation:

Salesperson: "Hello, Mr. Smith. This is Jim Londay with Londay Real Estate. I received a card in the mail today indicating your interest in a market evaluation of your house."
Prospect: "(affirmative answer)."

At this point, arrange your initial appointment using the same dialogue as described for a call-in prospect.

Levels of Motivation

The best response to get is from a person ready to market a house. This type of lead becomes your top priority and deserves your attention and best effort until his or her house is listed with you or someone else.

The next best response is from a Future File prospect, that is, a selling prospect not ready to sell his or her house immediately. It is beneficial to approach this person in the same way you would approach a person ready to list today. Motivations change without notice and today's "warm" prospects are often tomorrow's "hot" prospects. Many salespersons shun the prospect who is not ready to do business immediately. This attitude is costly. These property owners are the basis for building future listing volume and a healthy referral business.

Use the following steps with selling prospects not ready to list immediately:

1. Prepare and present a complete market analysis. Your new prospects will be impressed with your thoroughness and professionalism. They will appreciate your willingness to help, even though they are not ready to sell.
2. Send a handwritten thank-you note the day after you present your market analysis.
3. Add the prospect's name to your permanent file.
4. Include the prospect in your Future File, which consists of people expecting to sell their property in the near future.

The third type of response is from the person not contemplating any future property sale. He or she is merely interested in the current value of his or her house. Responses from this group are rare. For this group, prepare an abbreviated market analysis. Include sales of comparable properties, expireds, and current on-the-markets. If they wish, prepare a seller's estimate sheet. Briefly explain the different services you offer to homeowners. This presentation will be less extensive than that prepared for an immediate or Future File listing prospect. Be sure to mail thank-you notes and add the prospects' names to your permanent file. These people are an excellent source of referral business. In our society it is unusual and pleasant to find a person willing to provide a useful service for someone with no immediate gain in sight. Salespersons that provide service on this level are remembered and business will be sent their way.

Note: Refer to Chapter 6 for suggested procedures to use during your introductory appointment, Chapter 11 on how to service Future File prospects, and Chapter 12 on "Developing a Loyal Clientele."

Benefits of the Program

Exposure of Current Listings

Homeowners know more buying prospects for the neighborhood they live in than any other group of people. People wanting to move into a specific neighborhood often have friends or relatives already living there. By mailing a brochure to these people, you are bringing the property you have for sale to the attention of people likely to know a potential buyer. Tenants living in the same area as your listing will be among those contacted. In addition to knowing potential buyers for your property, they are also likely buying prospects. They have already demonstrated a preference for the area by the fact that they rented there. Direct mail in many cases will be the spark that lights the fire needed to transform them from complacent tenants into active buying prospects. By contacting these two groups of people, you are promoting your listing to buying prospects and people in contact with potential buyers you are unlikely to reach with other forms of advertising.

Promotion of You and Your Company

This program lets property owners know that your company and, more importantly, you personally are active in selling houses in their neighborhood. Your unique approach of promoting properties with direct mail will capture their attention. In many instances the Open House/Just Listed!/Just Sold! Program will be enough to get them to give you a call about handling the sale of their property or that of prospective sellers they know.

Servicing of Current Listings

A well-developed direct-mail program goes far beyond the normal advertising programs used in residential real estate sales. Sellers understand and appreciate that fact. It lets the sellers know that you are doing everything reasonably possible to find a buyer for their property and assures them you are working in their best interests.

Development of Listing Leads

The salesperson who makes 200 prospecting phone calls in the immediate neighborhood of each of his or her listings does not exist. It is not feasible to make even 50 calls every time you list a property. A well-designed direct-mail program directly offers your services to 200 families every time you list a house. That is prospecting!

Targeting of Advertising Dollars

Institutional advertising is an effective tool for large corporations like General Motors or Xerox. It is much less effective for a local real estate brokerage and not cost-effective at all for individual salespersons. Direct mail targets your precious advertising dollars to specific areas in which you are or would like to become established. A direct-mail piece with news about a person's neighborhood has a far greater impact than any other type of institutional or classified advertising.

Improvement of Listing Presentations

This program offers an unusual and effective advertising medium to prospective sellers. Brochures of previously sold properties in the selling prospect's neighborhood establish you as an area expert. Direct mail also provides you with an effective trial close. Prepare a brochure on the listing prospect's property and introduce it during the marketing segment of the listing presentation:

> "Mr. and Mrs. Seller, I've prepared a sample open house brochure for your property. Would you please look it over and make any suggestions you may have for improvements?"

Obtain approval and proceed as follows:

> "I can have this prepared and mailed in time for an open house on the 26th of this month. Would an open house on that date fit your schedule?"

Upon agreement on a date, open your appointment book and block out the open house date plus the date the brochures are to be mailed. This approach adds real punch and "close power" to listing presentations. (Note: This is only a small part of a properly prepared listing presentation. *See* Chapters 6 and 7.)

The Open House/Just Listed!/Just Sold! Program is a proven producer with multiple benefits. The most difficult aspect is getting it established. The program operates easily after you have your basic materials designed. You will be surprised at the many profitable benefits this program delivers. To ensure results, a salesperson starting this program should be committed to mailing at least 2,500 pieces of mail within one year of initiating the program and carefully research the areas to which he or she will mail to make sure there is market activity adequate to provide profitable results.

LOAN ASSUMPTION PROGRAM

When mortgage rates are high and sales are down, every salesperson dreams of having a large portfolio of listings, each with a great assumable loan. These listings are "money in the bank." But where do you find the prospects for these listings? The answer is simple. Direct your prospecting toward homeowners who bought their properties with FHA and VA loans during a period when interest rates were low. After a group of these prospects is identified, the most cost-effective and time-effective way to work them is by using a targeted direct-mail campaign.

Identifying Prospects

Your approach will depend on the system your multiple-listing service (MLS) uses. Your local MLS might publish a bound "sold" book every three, six, or 12 months. If so, choose the time frame you want and look up the index for each area of the city in which you are interested. Highlight and make a list of all final FHA and VA sales (*see* Example 18).

If your MLS does not publish this information in book form, you will have to rely on an alternative approach. All multiple-listing services provide some type of final sale information for appraisers. They may be individual one-quarter sheets on each sale, consisting of a photo of the property and all relevant listing and sale information. If your company does not subscribe to this service, you will need to solicit the help of an appraiser willing to let you research his or her records. The

Example 18

FINAL SALES INDEX

Address	List Price	Sale Price	Final/Fin	Rms	Baths	Gar	FP	Mort Bal	Date	Mkt Time
112 Mulberry	71,200	69,500	CO-OP – VA	7	2	2	1		3/7	42
1178 Harrison	64,950	64,950	CO-OP – LA	6	2	2	–	54,230	2/28	17
113811 Drexel	78,900	76,000	CO-OP – Conv	7	2	2	1		4/18	98
5001 Edinburg	84,500	83,000	LB – Conv	8	3	2	2		1/12	6
4526 Harrison	77,500	77,000	CO-OP – FHA	6	2	1	1		5/18	22
6733 So. 51st	54,000	54,000	LB – FHA	6	1	1	–		3/1	10
7714 So. 23rd	77,000	74,000	CO-OP – Conv	7	2	2	1		1/4	106
4412 Olive	92,000	90,000	LB – VA	8	3	2	2		4/23	77
5617 Galloway	65,000	62,000	LB – LA	6	1	2	–	48,678	3/1	12
6779 Oak	87,950	87,950	CO-OP – VA	7	2	2	1		4/30	88
12354 "B" St.	69,900	65,000	CO-OP – LA	5	2	2	–	46,392	1/20	66
7716 Virginia	77,950	76,000	LB – FHA	7	3	2	–		4/14	42
1947 So. 61st	98,000	96,000	LB – VA	7	2	3	1		2/2	1
453 Sunshine	72,900	72,000	CO-OP – FHA	6	2	2	–		5/15	53
7623 Warren	65,000	65,000	LB – VA	6	1	2	–		6/24	88
6789 Beales	82,000	79,000	LB – Conv	7	3	2	1		5/2	48
9826 Berry	77,500	72,000	CO-OP – FHA	6	2	1	–		3/30	77
7689 So. 44th	82,500	82,000	LB – LA	8	2	2	1	64,578	2/2	44
12658 Bay Dr	72,950	72,000	CO-OP – FHA	6	2	2	1		4/8	4
8954 Glasgow	88,950	86,000	LB – LA	7	2	2	1	54,678	6/22	66
8734 Byrne	74,500	74,500	CO-OP – VA	7	2	2	–		5/5	21
5746 Pine	66,500	65,000	LB – FHA	6	2	2	–		3/28	61
8345 "C"	64,900	62,000	CO-OP – LA	6	1	2	1		4/4	77
2388 So. 74	76,500	76,500	LB – VA	7	2	2	1		2/27	14

Example 19

Sample "Great Loan Assumption" Letter

LONDAY
Real Estate Company

Dear Homeowner:

You may be very fortunate and not know it! Multiple Listing
Service records indicate your house was purchased with FHA
or VA financing when rates were low.

Properties like yours, with good assumable loans, are bringing
a premimum in this time of high interest rates.

If you are considering selling or would merely like to know
what your house is worth in today's market, please contact me.
I'll prepare an analysis of your property informing you of
its approximate market value. In addition, I'll provide
statistics on current activity and answer any questions you
have. Of course, there is no cost or obligation.

If interested, please call, or fill in the enclosed card and
drop it in the mail. No postage is necessary.

Thanks for your time.

Sincerely,

Maureen Salesperson
Sales Associate

Bus: 555-5462
Res: 555-8361

Suite 402, Hillcrest Landing, Omaha, NE 68127
(402) 733-5443

prospect list you will obtain will be well worth the time you invest. Many multiple-listing services have or are instituting a computerized information bank. These systems are sophisticated and continually stockpile comprehensive data on market activity. Access to the information needed for this program through MLS computers will continue to increase and greatly simplify your research.

In most cases the sheer volume of prospects identified requires a direct-mail approach. There are usually too many potential prospects to contact by phone. I have had very good luck using a mass-produced mailer designed in letter form (Example 19). The only other enclosure was a business reply card. I identified more than 3,000 prospects spanning a two-year sales period in my market area. This number of prospects makes individual, personally addressed pieces impractical. Although it would probably increase your return somewhat to personally address these letters and envelopes, it would be too costly to look up 3,000 names in the reverse directory. When doing a mailing of this size, use "Resident" instead of the prospect's name on the envelopes.

As in all direct-mail programs, you can increase your yield by following up as many letters as possible with phone calls. A letter and follow-up phone call will always provide more prospects than either approach used exclusively. If you have identified fewer than 100 prospects, you may want to use the "Ten-and-Ten" Program explained later in this chapter. Here is a suggested dialogue for phone follow-ups:

Salesperson: "Hello, is Mr. Smith in?"
Prospect: "This is Mr. Smith."
S: "Mr. Smith, this is Jim Londay with Londay Real Estate Company. I recently mailed to you a letter detailing some of the services I have to offer. Have you had a chance to read it?"
P: "Yes, I have."
S: "Mr. Smith, my records indicate you bought your house with FHA financing in 19__. Is that correct?"
P: "Yes."
S: "As I mentioned in my letter, houses like yours are bringing a premium in today's market. Are you anticipating a move anytime in the next year?"

(Don't beat around the bush. Get to the point or risk losing the prospect without reaching first base.) If you receive an affirmative answer, proceed with the appointment-making process. If the prospects are not considering a move, ask them if they know of anyone else thinking of selling. Turn a negative answer into a positive lead. Consider every person you talk to as a possible source of listing leads. This type of contact will rarely provide you with leads if you do not ask for them.

Benefits of the Program

Provision of Salable Listing When Rates Are Up

This program increases in value and effectiveness whenever interest rates soar and the market deteriorates. It is the only prospecting program that generates increased income in a period of rising interest rates. This was brought home to me during a period of extremely high interest rates. When rates were at their highest, about 18 percent on fixed-rate first mortgages, properties with low-interest-rate, assumable FHA, VA, and Fannie Mae loans not only had little trouble selling but were commanding and getting a market value premium of ten to 20 percent! During this same period, houses with nonassumable loans were not selling or were selling with serious financial sacrifices borne by the sellers. Buydowns, discounted sales prices, and seller carrybacks with ridiculously low rates were carried to the extreme.

Adaptation to Market Situations

The lower the current financing rates are, the less effective this method becomes. However, you can make it work if you identify any period of time in the previous four to five years when first mortgage rates were three percent or more below the current rates. The greater the difference between current rates and the interest rate for the time period you are prospecting, the better the results will be.

Direction Toward High-Yield Prospects

Many houses sell within three to five years after they are purchased. Knowing this increases this program's effectiveness. Use your own judgment when deciding how far back you wish to go to identify prospects. When you go back more than five years, the program becomes less effective. After an extended period of time, owners are established in their homes and are less likely to put their homes on the market. Also, the farther back you go, the greater the seller's equity; this makes loan assumption sales more difficult to structure. Many buyers are unable to come up with the amount necessary to assume the loan if the equity is substantial; this requires you to go to workable but less-effective approaches such as wraparound mortgages and seller carrybacks.

Provision of Investment Opportunities

I am a strong advocate of buying real estate for investment purposes. Salespersons have an advantage over the average real estate investor in that they have greater access to good buys and can buy at a discount because they receive a commission on properties they buy for themselves.

By identifying and working loan assumption prospects, you will have the first opportunity to buy many attractive investment properties before they are placed on the open market. Thus, each prospect obtained with this program provides you with two opportunities: that of possibly earning a commission and that of buying an estate-building investment property. When buying investment property, be sure to disclose the fact that you are a licensed real estate agent. (Note: Check your state licensing laws to be sure you are in compliance with them when buying or selling property for yourself.)

Caveats

There is one aspect of selling houses on a loan assumption basis of which you need to make your sellers aware. If the buyer who assumed the loan defaults, the lending institution or the VA or FHA can go back to the original maker of the note for satisfaction.

This potential problem can be overcome by obtaining a release of liability from the FHA or VA. The cost is minimal. The only fee is a charge for a credit check. Frequently the lender servicing the loan will handle the paperwork for an additional fee. You can avoid the lender's processing fee by handling the paperwork yourself. To obtain a release, call the FHA or VA and ask them to mail a release-of-liability packet. Have the buyer and seller fill out the forms and mail them to the originating agency with a certified check or money order to cover the cost of a credit check. If the packet is approved by the FHA or VA, the original maker of the note (the owner letting his or her loan be assumed) is relieved of all liability if the purchaser defaults. I strongly recommend obtaining a release of liability on every property you sell on a loan assumption basis.

A related matter is the substitution of eligibility on VA loans. A person does not have to be a veteran to assume a VA loan. He or she must be a veteran, however, if the seller of the property wants to reacquire his or her eligibility when selling his or her property on a loan assumption basis. If a buyer has enough eligibility to substitute and is qualified in the eyes of the VA to purchase the house, it is a simple matter of again filling out the required forms and mailing them with a certified check for the credit check to the VA. An approved substitution of eligibility automatically provides the seller with a release of liability.

A VA assumption seller may decide that getting his or her eligibility back is not that important. In many cases he or she will not want to pass up a sale to a nonveteran assumption buyer and will only require a release of liability. The choice is the seller's. But it is your responsibility as the listing salesperson to explain the available options to any property owner considering letting a buyer assume his or her VA loan.

THE TEN-AND-TEN PROGRAM

The ten-and-ten program is a highly effective direct-mail program that can be used any time you have identified a list of prospects numbering between ten and 150 or more. It consists of mailing ten prospecting letters each Monday and following up each letter with a phone call later in the week.

Step One—Identify a Prospect List

The three groups of potential prospects mentioned earlier in the chapter: subdivisions five years old or less, starter areas, and neighborhoods going through a transition are all good candidates for this program. Last year's expireds (Chapter 4) will also provide you with a productive list of potential prospects.

Step Two—Prepare and Mail a Letter

Tailor the letter to the prospects' subdivision, neighborhood, or area of town. Keep it brief. It should be just long enough to describe your services, including the offer of a "no cost, no obligation" market analysis. Include a business reply card. After the letter is written and reproduced, address ten envelopes every Monday morning; insert copies of your letter, add postage, and drop them in the mail.

Step Three—The Follow-up Call

In your appointment book carry a list of the names and phone numbers of the ten prospects you mailed letters to on Monday. Starting Wednesday afternoon or evening, call each of the prospects on your list. Periodically call the remaining names on the list until you have talked to each of them. Use time that is normally nonproductive to make your calls. This includes: time sitting at the duty desk when the phone is not ringing; dead time between scheduled appointments; when waiting for the sales meeting to start; and any other time you have ten free minutes. By Friday or Saturday you should have contacted all of the people on your list.

Keep your follow-up call brief. Try this:

> "Mr. Smith, this is Jim Londay with Londay Real Estate Company. I mailed a letter to you on Monday. I'm calling to make sure you received it and to see if you have any questions or if I could help you with a real estate problem."

You will be pleasantly surprised by the number of solid listing prospects you will generate using this approach. If Mr. Smith is an immediate prospect, follow up as outlined in Chapters 6 and 7. If Mr. Smith is not an immediate prospect, thank him for his time and send him a brief handwritten thank-you note. Add his name to your newsletter list.

This program allows you to contact 500 potential prospects a year without scheduling an extra hour of work time. It will increase your "per hour" income. You will make more money without increasing your work hours.

BULK RATE MAIL

The main advantage of using the U.S. Post Office third-class bulk mail system is cost. Rates and corresponding savings vary depending on how you presort your mail. The best rates are less than one-half that of first-class mail. Another advantage is that you can have your bulk rate permit number printed on your envelopes at the same time you have your return address printed. This avoids the cost and hassle of buying, storing, and sticking stamps on hundreds of pieces of mail.

The post office offers a basic third-class bulk rate with two progressive levels of discounts beyond the basic rate. The first discount level past the basic rate is given for presorting by zip code and requires more than ten pieces per zip to qualify for the discount. A further discount is available for addressing your mail by carrier route.

Two postal permits are needed to operate these programs. The first is a bulk mail permit, which allows you to mail using third-class bulk mail rates. The second is a business reply permit, which allows you unlimited distribution of business reply cards. Both of these postal permits are good for one calendar year starting January 1. The cost of both permits is moderate and will be recovered in reduced postage savings in your first few mailings. You can distribute as many business reply cards as you like without owing a postage fee to the post office. Postage on business reply mail is charged only on cards actually mailed to and received by the permit holder. It is a small cost for the benefit received (*see* Examples 20 and 21).

Your first step in setting up your direct-mail program will be to contact the postal permits department. They have the information, forms, and materials you need to get started and will be able to answer specific questions regarding procedures. The employees in the bulk mail department of the post office are among the most helpful and cooperative of all public service employees. Once you are familiar with the bulk mail system, you will find it efficient, easy to use, and cost-effective.

Example 20

BUSINESS REPLY PERMIT APPLICATION

U.S. POSTAL SERVICE
APPLICATION TO MAIL WITHOUT AFFIXING POSTAGE STAMPS

APPLICANT: File at office where mailings will be made with required fee.

NAME OF APPLICANT *(Print or type)*	APPLICANT'S TELEPHONE NO.

ADDRESS OF APPLICANT *(Street, Apt./Suite No., City, State and ZIP Code) (Print or Type)*

AVERAGE NUMBER OF PIECES IN EACH MAILING	CLASS OF MAIL MATTER ☐ FIRST ☐ SECOND ☐ THIRD ☐ FOURTH	SIGNATURE OF APPLICANT	DATE

TO BE COMPLETED ▶ BY POSTMASTER	AMOUNT OF FEE COLLECTED $	PERMIT NUMBER	DATE OF ISSUANCE

POSTMASTER: Retain application in your file. When approved, deliver authorization to permit holder.

PS Form 3601, July 1980

U.S. POSTAL SERVICE
AUTHORIZATION TO MAIL WITHOUT AFFIXING POSTAGE STAMPS

You are authorized to mail at this post office matter bearing permit imprints, postage to be paid in money.

POST OFFICE *(City, State and ZIP Code)*

PERMIT NUMBER	DATE OF ISSUANCE	SIGNATURE OF POSTMASTER

NAME OF PERMIT HOLDER *(Address, Apt./Suite No., City, State and ZIP Code)*

TO:

PS Form
July 1980 **3601**

Example 21

BULK MAIL PERMIT APPLICATION

FORM 3614, BRM APPLICATION AND ANNUAL RENEWAL NOTICE

Application is made to distribute business reply cards, envelopes, self mailers, cartons, and labels prepared and mailed for return without prepayment of postage under Section 917, Domestic Mail Manual. Postage at First-Class rates and the additional per piece charge for business reply mail will be paid on all pieces returned under this privilege. Applicant agrees to prepare mailing pieces in accordance with Section 917, Domestic Mail Manual, and understands that failure to conform with those requirements may be considered basis for revocation of this permit. The annual business reply permit fee, and the annual accounting charge if payment is to be from a BRM trust account, must accompany this request.

PERMIT MUST BE RENEWED BY DECEMBER 31. BRM WILL NOT BE DELIVERED WITHOUT A VALID PERMIT.

NAME AND ADDRESS OF PERMIT HOLDER (print or type)	NAME		TELEPHONE NO.
	STREET	CITY AND STATE	ZIP CODE
POST OFFICE TO WHICH SUBMITTED (City, State and ZIP Code)	SIGNATURE AND TITLE OF APPLICANT		DATE

TO BE COMPLETED BY POSTMASTER

BRM ACCOUNT YES NO	BRM ACCOUNT FEE RECEIPT NO.	BRM PERMIT FEE RECEIPT NO.	☐ APPLICATION APPROVED ☐ APPLICATION DENIED	PERMIT NUMBER
DATE OF ISSUANCE	DATE OF EXPIRATION	SIGNATURE OF POSTMASTER		

● POSTMASTER MUST GIVE CUSTOMER FORM 3544, RECEIPT FOR PAYMENT FOR PROOF OF HAVING A VALID PERMIT.

BILLING CODE 7710-12-C

FORM SIZE 3 7/8" X 8"

CHAPTER 4

WORKING EXPIRED LISTINGS

If you thrive on competition and are self-motivated, expired listings are for you. Expired listings are the promised land for goal-oriented salespersons. If direct mail is looked upon as a "shotgun" approach to prospecting, then working expireds can be likened to using a rifle with a high-powered scope. Diligently working expired listings is the quickest way to build up your listing portfolio.

THE NATURE OF EXPIREDS

Many factors affect the real estate marketplace. Changes in interest rates, the economy, seller and buyer attitudes, and a multitude of other factors form the basis for a constantly changing marketplace. In residential real estate sales, we face a new ballgame every day.

In spite of these constant changes, every property is salable if marketed correctly. Every real estate listing that ever expired went unsold during the listing period because, based on its location, its condition, and the financing terms, it was overpriced. All factors that can cause a property to not sell are a function of price. If it did not sell, based on all the factors involved, the price was too high. This is an absolute truth of the marketplace. After you understand why properties did not sell when they should have, working expireds is a relatively simple undertaking. Knowledgeable salespersons understand the workings of the marketplace and strive to market expired listings at either a reduced price, in better condition, or with financing terms significantly better than when the property was last on the market. At times an adjustment will be needed in only one area. At other times a combination, or even all three areas will need adjustments to make the property salable.

The fact that you, the salesperson, know how the marketplace works and why a property did not sell is just the first step in being successful at working expireds. It is your ability to get sellers to understand how basic marketing principles work and how they relate to their particular situation that will turn you into a salesperson who gets listings sold quickly on a regular basis.

Another advantage of working this group of prospects is that expired listings that are placed back on the market at a competitive price, condition, and terms have a much shorter average marketing time than properties listed for the first time. This factor increases your income potential because less of your time will be needed before the sale is made.

The moneymaking potential of working expireds creates competition among aggressive salespeople. The very nature of expireds draws hungry salespeople to them. Working expireds is not for the weak-willed or easily discouraged; however, if you learn the basics and consistently apply your knowledge, the rewards are great. Working expireds takes more immediate effort but provides more immediate results than any other type of prospecting. Forget what the competition is doing. After you learn how to work expireds, and work them aggressively, you will get more than your share of the possible listings. Conduct your business so that the competition worries about you, and you will not have to worry about them.

If you are new to working expireds, your first step is to become familiar with the rules established by your local MLS or Board of REALTORS® and any state licensing laws designed to protect the rights of the original listing salesperson and broker. Avoid going "behind the sign" or violating local standard practices. Being assertive and playing the game hard is accepted by fellow professionals. Learn what the acceptable standards of conduct are in your locale and adopt them as your personal standard. Do not legally or ethically violate the rights of a previous listing broker or salesperson.

There are three basic steps in working expireds. The first is identifying owners of expired listings. The second is contacting each prospect as soon as it is physically, legally, and ethically possible. The last is getting the appointment, persuading the sellers that you are the best salesperson to get their property sold, and then listing their property. We will look at each of these steps.

IDENTIFYING PROSPECTS

The approach used in identifying new expireds will depend on the method by which your local MLS updates and releases this information to its members.

If Your MLS Is Computerized

Many MLSs now process and disseminate their listings and all related data through a central computer. Individual salespersons in this system have access to information through stationary or portable computer terminals in their offices or homes. Under this type of program, expireds usually are released daily. In many computer programs the expireds appear in different search modes of the computer at different times in the day. You will need to determine where they appear first to avoid losing prospects to competing salespersons. The best source of this information is the programmer of the system or the MLS employee in charge of its daily operation.

If Your MLS Is Noncomputerized

In a noncomputerized MLS, the expireds usually are released daily or weekly in printed form. In some systems the new expireds are lumped together with those previously released. If this is so in your system, you will have the added step of separating the newly expired listings from the old. This extra step washes out many salespersons who would like to work expireds but balk at the extra work.

The frequency with which expireds are released in a paperwork-based system will determine how much time will be required to properly research and contact each owner. At one time the MLS I was affiliated with released this information weekly. The volume of new prospects was so great that it took two to three days to work all of them. This is a considerable investment of time but I averaged over two new listings a week using this one source.

In working expireds under any type of system there is a direct relationship between how quickly you contact the available prospects and your ratio of success. In many instances 30 minutes means the difference between success and failure when approaching an easily located owner because you probably will not be the only salesperson trying to contact that prospective seller. It is important to be prepared and ready to work when the new expireds are released. Being the first salesperson in the door when working expireds pays financial dividends.

Rating the Prospects

After obtaining your list of prospects, rate them by their desirability. The quickest way is to look each of them up in a recent MLS book. Write down the order in which you are going to work them, considering location, apparent condition, asking price/market value ratio and the available financing of each property. Generally houses that appear as if they should have already sold provide the best opportunities. Concentrate your initial efforts on their owners.

I advocate working every expired prospect you identify. The only exceptions are properties owned by licensed real estate salespersons or brokers. The reason most salespersons fail when working expireds is that they do not persist long enough to find the "impossible-to-find" owners. If finding the prospect takes any real effort, they give up. The hard-to-find prospects are where the real money is to be made.

HARD-TO-SELL PROPERTIES

Overpriced properties and properties with incurable defects are the two categories of properties you will most likely encounter. Overpriced properties provide a golden opportunity to salespersons who understand the nature of expireds. In the case of many expired listings, the fact that the property is overpriced is not the property owner's fault. The number of owners of expired listings who initially overpriced their property on the basis of their original listing salesperson's advice is amazing. "Buying" listings by promising unrealistically high sales prices is common. In many of these cases the owners knew their properties were overpriced but were waiting for their salespersons to advise them on needed changes.

Work each of the overpriced prospects hard until you can determine if the owner is firm in his or her resolve to get more for the property than it is worth. If the motivation to sell is there, all you need to do is to show the sellers the reduced-price path to success.

Properties with incurable defects are the other type of expired listing prospect from which most salespersons shy away. Examples are houses with poor locations (next to an industrial plant or on a busy street), design problems (a four-bedroom house with one bathroom), or site problems (a steeply pitched driveway). In most cases the only cure for a defect of this type is a significant reduction in price. Every property has a buyer if it is priced and promoted properly. Do not fall into the trap of thinking that just because you would not want to buy a property, no one else would. After all, the owner of the industrial plant may need additional office space or additional parking.

These leads should be dropped only after it is apparent that the seller lacks sufficient motivation to make the concessions necessary to get the property sold. The best approach to working with these sellers is the "you bought at a discount because of the defect, you are going to have to offer the property at a discount in order to sell" technique (*see* Chapter 8, "Obtaining Price, Terms, and Condition Adjustments"). Work the owners of these properties last, as time permits. But be sure to work them, as your greatest success will come when you work *all* expireds until they are listed or lost.

LOCATING THE PROSPECTS

Who Is the Owner?

Determining who the owner is and finding him or her before another salesperson does is the next step in working expireds. Prepare yourself by obtaining current issues of all cross-reference and reverse directories for your area. The Polk Directory and the telephone system reverse street directory are usually available. The Polk gives the most complete information on each resident including his or her status as a homeowner or tenant.

The phone company reverse street directory is usually more current but contains less detailed information. Having a copy of every available directory is important because in many cases the information needed to find an owner will be found in only one source. Directories from previous years will also prove valuable on occasion.

The following sources are the most commonly used in locating the owners of expired listings:

1. Home phone,
2. Neighbors,
3. Tenants,
4. Courthouse/title companies,
5. Post office, and
6. Relatives.

These sources are not always worked in this order. At times you will need to try a number of sources before obtaining the name of the property owner or some other piece of information that will lead you to the owner.

Home Phone Number

Finding the owner's home phone number and calling him or her is the normal starting point. Calling this number will tell you a lot. If the number is in service, you know that the owner still is living in the house or has moved to another location in the immediate area and will be easy to find. If the number has been changed, you know that the owner has moved from the house but still is living locally. If disconnected with no forwarding telephone number, you know that the seller probably has moved out of town, which means you need to try another approach.

If you are lucky enough to catch one of the owners at home, start a conversation and proceed into the appointment-making process as described later in this chapter. If a child, baby-sitter, relative, or any person other than the owner answers the phone, try to obtain a number at which the owner can be contacted. If at all possible, do not wait until the owner comes home to make your initial contact. If the owners are not at a place where they can be contacted, find out when they will be home and call them promptly at that time. Do not rely on the seller to return your call. You can, however, leave your name and number and take a chance that they will come home early and are the type of people who promptly return calls.

If there is no answer at the home number, keep trying periodically as you work the other expired listings. Try as often as time permits, every 15 or 30 minutes if possible or until you have contacted the owner through another approach.

Neighbors

Contacting neighbors is often productive when the prospect cannot be found at home or work or in the event the prospect has moved, leaving a disconnected phone with no forwarding number. Using a reverse directory, contact all neighbors on either side or across the street from the prospect's address. Do not give up until you have contacted all the neighbors within five houses of your prospect's property or until you have hit pay dirt and found out how to contact your prospect. If the property is particularly attractive, it is worth canvassing the entire street the prospect lives on in an effort to find him or her.

Try the following approach:

"Mrs. Smith, this is Jim Londay, with Londay Real Estate Company. I am trying to locate Warren Baker, the owner of the house next door (down the street, around the corner) to you. Would you happen to have his new address or phone number?"

If Mrs. Smith is hesitant, tell her you need to contact Mr. Baker in a matter regarding the sale of his house and that you are quite sure he would want her to help you out if she could. Take either a phone number or address.

If the neighbors you contact do not have specific information that will help, see if they know the city to which your prospect has moved in the event the owner has left the city. You can call long-distance information to that city and ask for a new listing under the prospect's name. This technique proves effective in a large number of cases and should be used whenever the seller is no longer in town and you cannot get an exact phone number or address.

If the neighbors you talk to do not know what city the prospect has moved to, ask if they know any friend or relative of the prospect who may help you. In some instances, a neighbor will be unwilling to give you information but will direct you to someone else who can help. Use the conversation to try and develop other leads. Take this opportunity to inquire about other possible current or future selling prospects in the neighborhood. This approach multiplies the possibility of obtaining a listing from each phone contact.

If the neighbors provide you with any helpful information, send them handwritten thank-you notes and a business card. Also include one of the business reply cards described in the chapter on direct-mail prospecting. If any of these people are possible future prospects or referral sources, add them to your permanent file (*see* Chapter 12, "Developing a Loyal Clientele").

Tenants

The easiest approach to finding out who the owner of a rental property is and how he or she can be found is through a present or past tenant. Normally you can determine if the occupant is a tenant by looking up the property in the MLS as it was listed by the previous salesperson. Obtain the tenant's name and number from a reverse directory. When calling, use dialogue similar to:

> "Mr. Johnson, this is Jim Londay with Londay Real Estate Company. I understand that you are currently renting (previously rented) the house located at 4110 Misty Lane. I am trying to contact your landlord concerning the status of the sale of the property. Could you please tell me how to get in touch with him or her?"

After you have the needed information, determine if the tenant is a buying prospect:

> "Mr. Johnson, as you know, the owner of the house you are renting has been actively trying to sell it. Are you considering buying a home if you decide to move?"

Tenants are excellent buying prospects. In many cases they are ready to purchase a house if approached correctly. At times they are buying prospects for the very house they are renting. Take these opportunities to develop potential buyers and increase your sales volume.

Courthouse or Title Companies

In some instances you will be unable to find the property owner's name through researching directories or calling neighbors or tenants. In these cases obtain an "owner of record" through the courthouse or a title company. Some courthouses will give owner-of-record information over the phone. Many will not.

If this information cannot be obtained by calling the courthouse, you will need to solicit help from a title company. Many title companies will provide this information over the phone at no cost to their regular customers. In fact some title companies have employees on duty during working hours at the courthouse and can provide you with information on short notice. Services offered by title companies vary and there may be a fee for this service in your area. By finding and working with a cooperative title company, you will shorten the time you need to locate prospects. After you have the name of the owner of record, go back to your directory sources or neighbors to get a phone number or address.

Post Office

The post office provides two services that will help you locate an owner who has moved. First, a forwarding address can be obtained by visiting the post office that delivers mail to the address of the expired listing. This provides a forwarding address in the shortest possible time but requires a trip to the post office. The post office will not release this information over the phone.

At times you will have immediate prospects to work and will not have time to drive to the post office. In this instance send an envelope addressed to the property owners at their old address. Type the words "address correction requested" on the lower lefthand corner of the envelope. The post office will return the envelope to you with the owner's new address. This allows you to obtain a phone number through directory service and contact the prospects with a long-distance phone call. If the property has not yet been listed, this phone call and subsequent conversation in most cases will give you the listing. If the prospect has no phone or has an unlisted number, follow up using a letter.

Relatives

This is a last-ditch approach and will work only if the elusive prospect has an unusual last name. Call people in the phone book with the same last name as your property owner. With luck you will find a relative who will be able to provide you with an address or phone number. Try this approach:

> "Mr. Oddname, this is Jim Londay with Londay Real Estate Company. I am trying to contact Larry Oddname regarding the sale of his house on Apricot Court. Could you please tell me where I could locate him?"

If the relative is reluctant, explain in detail why you are trying to contact him. If Mr. Oddname is related to the prospect, he will in almost all instances give you the information you need. I have found many otherwise impossible-to-find sellers in this way. Remember, the true professional forges ahead, applies these techniques, and succeeds.

Be like a bloodhound when tracking down hard-to-find owners. Locating these property owners provides a surprising rate of success. Some instances in which it took nearly two weeks to locate what I thought were marginal prospects resulted in listings and subsequent sales. Work the difficult cases diligently. They provide the best opportunity for salespersons who are not easily discouraged. Carry on when the others fail, and you will win.

CATEGORIZING PROSPECTS

Owners of expireds fall into three main categories. The first is the owner who has not relisted his or her property, still wants to sell at the present time, and is not committed to another salesperson. These prospects are your first priority. Put everything else, including lunch and your tennis game, on the back burner until such a prospect is listed with you or someone else.

The second type of seller is still interested in selling but plans to take his or her house off the market for the present. In this instance make an appointment and visit with the owner in person. Satisfy yourself that the owner is not an immediate prospect. Many of these prospects still have the motivation to sell their property immediately and are only taking it off the market because they feel the property presently is unsalable. If you feel the property can be sold now with correct marketing and can get the seller to see your reasoning, he or she will often decide to place the house back on the market immediately. An appointment gives you a chance to introduce yourself and begin building a relationship even if the prospect does decide to wait until later to place the property back on the market. Your end goal is, of course, the listing of his or her property when he or she decides to sell. If the owners decide to wait, add them to your Future File (*see* Chapter 11, "The Future File").

The third category includes sellers who have already renewed their original listings, listed with new salespersons, or made unshakable commitments to someone other than you. In most cases drop such a prospect and move to the next one on your list. However, if the seller volunteers the date his or her extension or new listing expires, make a note of it and ask if you can contact him or her then if the property is still unsold. Follow up with a thank-you note and place the date you can call him or her on your calendar.

CONTACTING PROSPECTS

Initial Telephone Contact

When making your initial contact, identify yourself and establish why you are calling. Use a dialogue like this:

> "Mr. Seller, this is Jim Londay with Londay Real Estate Company. According to Multiple-Listing Service records, your listing with XYZ Company has expired. Are you still interested in selling your house?"

Getting quickly to the point avoids wasting everyone's time. You will be surprised at the number of people who are unaware that their listings have expired. Frequently the original listing salesperson has not contacted the seller about an extension or even picked up the sign and lockbox.

The Key Question

After it has been established that the previous listing has expired and the prospect has told you that he or she is still interested in selling, control the conversation by asking a series of questions based on their motivation, where they are moving, and how the property was previously marketed. Develop the conversation to the point where you can comfortably ask what I call the "key question." One key question will open the door to success in working expired listings to the salesperson who knows how to ask it and follow up on it properly. Part of its effectiveness lies in its simplicity. The question is,

"Mr. Seller, why do you feel your house hasn't sold?"

It does not sound like much but it is.

The key question serves three very important functions. First, it gives your prospect an opportunity to vent what in many cases is months of built-up frustrations. After three or four months of having his or her house on the market, the seller needs somebody new to talk to about the woeful situation. This question usually opens the floodgates. You will hear every imaginable reason why the property did not sell: high interest rates, not enough advertising, listed with the wrong company, previous listing salesperson did not try, plus an assortment of others. Whether or not the seller is correct, the key question has served its first purpose: providing a relief valve for the seller.

The second function is to give you a basis upon which to ask questions and build dialogue. As in all sales situations, the person asking the questions controls the conversation. Ask a series of questions based on whatever the prospect tells you. The seller's response to these questions will open the door to appointment-making opportunities. You will find a list of suggested questions in Chapter 5, "Working For-Sale-by-Owners." You do not have to agree with the prospect's reasoning. You can respond by saying,

"I understand how you feel. If I were in your situation, I probably would view your problem the same way."

Whatever the prospect's response, use it as a base upon which to develop your conversation.

The third function is that of actually providing a reason for making an appointment. After the initial response to the key question and the following discussion, the seller will frequently ask you why you think his or her house did not sell. Even if you know the reason, do not tell the owner over the phone. Respond by saying:

"Because I've never been in your house, Mr. Seller, I can't give you an informed opinion. However, if I can have

45 minutes of your time, I will be able to tell you exactly
why your property did not sell. I will also provide you with
suggestions on what needs to be done to increase the salability of your property."

On occasion, a prospect will ask why you did not show the
property when it was on the market. Inform the seller that you
carry a relatively large portfolio of listings and that you devote
the majority of your time to promoting and showing the properties you, not other salespersons, have listed. The prospect will
have a particularly strong positive reaction if he or she feels the
previous salesperson did not work hard enough for them.

Offering a no-cost analysis of why the property did not sell
is the most effective approach you can use to obtain an appointment. If they do not ask for your opinion on why it did not sell,
it is up to you to bring up the subject. Say something like this:

"Mr. Seller, I understand your frustration. With your
permission, I would like to visit with you this morning or
afternoon. I'll look at your house and review what has been
done to date to sell it. After that, I will be able to tell you
why it didn't sell and make some specific recommendations
that will help the house sell when you decide to put it back
on the market."

Set an appointment. In most cases the owner of an expired
listing will give the subsequent listing to the first competent
salesperson he or she sees after the original agreement lapses.
Schedule the appointment for immediately after your initial
phone conversation if possible. Make every effort to be the first
salesperson there.

Sometimes an owner will be reluctant to set an appointment. Do not let this deter you. You have made good progress
in finding the seller, establishing the fact that he or she is a
prospect, and introducing yourself. If you do not get the appointment, all your work to this point will be lost. Remember that
most sellers in this situation have heard all the baloney and
runaround they will ever need. Their reluctance at this point
can often be overcome by assuring them that their problems
can be solved with the correct marketing approach. Make sure
that the prospect understands that there is no cost or obligation.

Using the key question and following up correctly should
result in seeing the owner in the majority of cases in which you

are talking to a valid prospect. You will need to change your dialogue and/or tone of approach if you frequently are unable to get an appointment. Pinpoint the problem area in your approach by reviewing every unsuccessful phone contact as soon as it is over. Look for a pattern. If necessary, review the circumstances with your manager or a fellow salesperson whose judgment you trust. Ask fellow salespeople for wording they have found to be effective in the same situation. The key to success in working the phone is in constantly refining your dialogue and manner of speaking.

APPOINTMENT PREPARATION

You have made the appointment for the earliest possible time, in many cases within an hour or two of the initial phone conversation. You will have little time to prepare your presentation. Be ready by assembling presentation folders in advance. Include all presentation materials you normally use. (*See* Chapter 6, "Preparing the Listing Presentation".) Include blank seller's estimate sheets and listing agreements with carbons.

You will need to collect current market data to be fully prepared. If your comparable file is up-to-date, you should be able to gather the necessary final sales, pendings, expireds, and current on-the-markets in 20 or 30 minutes. Assemble this with your previously prepared packet. Bring this packet along with your tape measure and anything else you will need to list the property. This is normally the only time you prospect for listings in which you want to list the property without completing a prior measure-up appointment as described in Chapter 6.

Owners of expired listings are looking for results. They still own a house they thought would be sold by now. Let the prospect know you are there for one purpose, to solve their unsold-house problem. In all forms of prospecting, real estate salespersons must realize that they are in a form of show business. Substance alone will impress no one unless it is packaged and presented properly. This is especially true when meeting owners of expired listings for the first time.

After introducing yourself, get to work immediately by making a deliberate, fact-finding tour of the property. Check it out thoroughly. Ask a lot of questions. Take more time than you really need to learn what you need to know about the property itself. Take a few pages of notes. You will have a solid basis on which to make recommendations and the seller will know in a tangible way that you have checked out the property sufficiently to tell them why it did not sell. You will have a chance to learn your seller's situation, concerns, and motivations. Do not volunteer any of your thoughts during the tour of the property. Do your presentation immediately if all owners are present at the initial visit. If one of the owners is not home, make an appointment for that evening or as soon as you can meet all the owners at one time.

PRESENTATION DIALOGUE

After touring the house and gathering the data you need, set the stage for your presentation:

> "Mr. and Mrs. Johnson, before leaving the office, I collected some information on recent sales activity in your neighborhood. If you have a few minutes, I would like to share it with you and explain how it relates to your situation. I also would like to briefly share some basic marketing principles that will help you understand why your house hasn't sold."

Suggest sitting down at a table where you can lay out your materials. Start by giving a brief overview of real estate marketing principles. Briefly explain the different market forces that determine what sells and when (*see* "Setting the Stage" in Chapter 7, "Getting the Listing"). Proceed with the listing presentation as outlined in Chapter 6 until after presenting the final solds and current on-markets you have assembled. This is the critical moment when you tell the owners why the property did not sell. Hesitancy or any uncertainty on your part now will destroy your credibility. You must convey the fact that you know why the property did not sell and that you know what it will take to get it sold. This should not be an act. It is a basic marketing fact that if a property does not sell, based on its location, condition, and financing terms offered, the price is too high. And that is exactly what you are going to tell the prospects.

Tell them what the specific problems are on their property. List them on a tablet you have brought with you for that purpose. Next, outline what you feel the seller needs to do to get the property sold. Also list these on the tablet. In almost all cases, your suggestions will include a price adjustment and/or improving the condition of the property.

After making specific recommendations, prepare a seller's estimate sheet based on your suggested offering price. Include the cost of any improvements you want them to complete. Take charge. These prospects are looking for your guidance. Use the following trial close: Turn the seller's estimate sheet toward the owners and go over each entry. When you get to the bottom, circle the estimated net figure and ask:

> "Mr. and Mrs. Seller, would a sale giving you this approximate net be acceptable?"

Give them plenty of time and be sure to let them speak first. The silence may be awkward for you but will be intolerable for them. After you agree on a satisfactory net figure, proceed as outlined in Chapter 7, "Getting the Listing," to actually get the prospect to place the property on the market before you leave the house.

THE OUT-OF-TOWN SELLER

Listing an expired property whose owner is living out-of-town is an art in itself. After contacting the owner on the phone and establishing that the owner meets all the criteria of a valid prospect, prepare a written proposal and send it at once using Express Mail or one of the overnight mail-delivery services. This creates urgency, makes a positive impression, and is worth the cost.

Your packet should include all materials normally used in your listing presentation. Briefly explain the contents with a cover letter that includes your specific recommendations regarding pricing and improving the condition of the property. Stress the importance price, terms, and condition play in the salability of a property. Close your letter with a request that the owner call you collect immediately upon receipt of your packet. You can then answer any questions and have a chance to obtain a commitment.

Be sure to include a prepaid Express Mail or overnight delivery service envelope in your packet. This creates more urgency and a sense of obligation. A competing salesperson will be unlikely to go to this extent to try to obtain the listing. In most cases you will obtain the listing by default if the out-of-town seller is not already committed to another salesperson.

Working with owners of expireds has many advantages. Having been unsuccessful in selling their property while it was listed with other salespersons, these owners usually are highly motivated and more realistic about what their property is worth than when they first went on the market. In most cases they are ready to accept advice from a real estate salesperson who they feel can get the job done. An additional benefit is that these owners are already committed to the idea of listing with a salesperson, a definite advantage over working FSBOs.

LAST YEAR'S EXPIREDS

An excellent project for the cold winter months when you are likely to have time on your hands consists of researching the previous year's multiple-listing records to identify listings that expired and were not placed on the market again and sold. The next step is to locate and contact the owners of these properties to determine if they are valid selling prospects for the present year.

This approach works best in January, February, and March. In many instances owners of houses that do not sell by fall get discouraged and take their property off the market for the winter. Many of these owners still would like to sell their houses and are ready to list when springtime arrives. They are a high-yield category of prospects.

Identify the Prospects

Pick a multiple-listing area you wish to work. Using the MLS computer or printed sold records, list all the expired listings for that area for the previous year. Using a one-year-old directory and the most current directory, cross-check the listings for an address to see if the same resident is listed in both directories. If so, the house probably was not sold and the owners are prime, high-yield selling prospects.

Use a phone, mail, or combination approach. The widespread geographical location of the properties makes in-person, door-knocking contacts impractical in most cases. A phone or

mail approach may be used. The "Ten-and-Ten" Program outlined in Chapter 3 is a good choice.

Phone Approach

Best results are obtained by getting to the point promptly when
making the initial phone call. Try the following:

> Prospect: "Hello."
> Agent: "Hello, is Mr. or Mrs. Hagge there, please?"
> P: "This is Mr. Hagge."
> A: "Mr. Hagge, this is Jim Londay with Londay Real
> Estate Co. I've been reviewing my multiple-listing records
> and noticed your property was on the market last year but
> was not sold. Is that correct?"
> P: "Yes."
> A: "Mr. Hagge, are you interested in selling if a buyer
> could be found for your house at the right price and terms?"

After you have determined that you are talking to valid prospects, gauge their motivation and tailor your response as outlined earlier in this chapter.

Mail Approach

Use the mail if you identify too many prospects to contact by
telephone. Use individually typed and addressed letters mailed
first class. Type these letters during what would normally be
downtime for you or your secretary to make the most of nonproductive time while not disturbing your normal routine.

If individually typed letters are not feasible because you
have identified an unusually large number of prospects, use a
mass-produced form letter (Example 22). While not as effective
as a personalized letter, it is still effective, especially if followed
up with a phone call. Including a business reply card will
increase your yield by making it easy for the prospect to contact
you.

Working last year's expireds is a great way to build your
listing portfolio in the first three months of the year. Plant seeds
in January that are harvested in June.

Example 22   **SAMPLE "Last Year's Expired" Letter**

LONDAY
Real Estate Company

Dear Homeowner:

According to Multiple Listing Service records, your house was on the market, but was not sold during the past year. If still interested in selling, I would like to prepare a no cost, no obligation market analysis of your property. Included will be:

1) An estimate of the present market value of your house.

2) The estimated net proceeds resulting from a sale at that price.

3) A detailed marketing plan designed to produce a sale at top dollar in the shortest time possible.

If interested, please call me, or fill in the enclosed card and drop in the mail. No postage is necessary.

Thanks for your time and interest.

Sincerely,

Greg Salesperson
Sales Associate

Bus: 555-1034
Res: 555-4026

Suite 402, Hillcrest Landing, Omaha, NE 68127
(402) 733-5443

CHAPTER 5

WORKING FOR-SALE-BY-OWNERS

For-sale-by-owners (FSBOs) are a prime source of listing prospects for a number of reasons. The motivation of property owners trying to sell their own property is evident. The time-consuming process of wading through dozens or hundreds of nonprospects while phone canvassing or knocking on doors to find someone interested in selling is eliminated. With the exception of working expireds, FSBOs are the fastest way for salespersons to fatten up their "current listings" files.

Working FSBOs is not easy. The competition for these prospects can be stiff. Another factor is that seller resistance to listing property with a salesperson is stronger with FSBOs than with any other group of listing prospects and is the cause of the significant and frequent time lag between the initial contact with these prospects and the time they finally list. This is in marked contrast to working expireds, who are normally listed within a day or two of first contact. This chapter explains how to overcome these potential roadblocks in a logical, effective manner, thereby giving you another approach that can be used to increase your listing volume.

LOCATING FSBO PROSPECTS

Homeowners trying to sell their own property have a limited number of ways in which they can advertise and promote their property. Their advertisements are the source of most FSBO listing leads. The principal source of prospects is the classified

77

ad section of your local newspaper. Most people trying to sell their own property try to generate buyers through newspaper ads. Check the papers daily to keep current with what is being offered on the FSBO market.

Other good sources are local shopper papers or advertising magazines devoted to real estate. Many salespersons find public bulletin boards in grocery stores, beauty and barber shops, industrial lunchrooms, etc., to be fertile grounds for locating FSBO prospects. In some locales, there are advertising circulars devoted entirely to advertising FSBO properties. They usually are distributed at no cost at grocery stores and other outlets. These can be a real boon to salespersons. Pick up one of these and you have more prospects than you can contact in a week!

The last principal source of prospects is yard signs. Any FSBO signs you notice in your everyday travels should be added to your active prospect file.

Get in the habit of checking these sources daily and you will have an abundance of high-yield prospects.

Organize a for-sale-by-owner file. Start by keeping a master index-card file of all current FSBO prospects. I file FSBO prospect cards by phone number rather than by name. Many times the only reference point in an FSBO ad is a phone number. When I scan the paper I can check the phone number and see if a prospect is already in my file. This eliminates going through reverse directories only to find that you already have placed that prospect in your card file. After the initial contact is made, label a file folder and start keeping comprehensive notes on every contact you have with the prospect. You are in business to see prospects, not keep books. Keep your system simple or it will consume too much of your valuable time.

OPENING DIALOGUE

Knocking on the door and introducing yourself in person is the best approach when making your first contact with FSBO prospects. Unless you are exceptionally good on the phone, you will find real progress with FSBOs hard to come by using a phone approach. The optimum length of your initial contact will be determined by the reaction you receive from the prospect. This is another judgment call. You certainly do not want to give up too soon but you want to stop short of offending the prospect.

Definitely stay past the introduction phase. After introducing yourself as a salesperson, gain control of the conversation by asking a series of questions. If you ask the right questions you will be doing little talking but will be in nearly complete control of the conversation. Here are some examples:

"Mr. Seller, you have a lovely home. May I ask what you have priced it at?"

"How did you arrive at that price?"

"How long has it been on the market?"

"Are you satisfied with the market activity you have had to date?"

"Are you changing locations in the city or are you planning a long-distance move?" (If they are moving out of town, apply the "out-of-town reference technique" as outlined in Chapter 6.)

"What type of financing terms are you offering?"

"Do you understand how discount points work?"

"Do you understand how to qualify buyers for different types of financing?"

"Have you arranged for an attorney to write the purchase agreement if and when you find a buyer?"

Use the responses to these questions as a basis for discussion. Mentally catalog the prospect's answers. Each of the areas in which the selling prospect is not well versed will provide you with a valid reason for a follow-up visit during which you will provide him or her with materials and/or information in the areas in which the prospect lacks knowledge. You will do this because: **For-sale-by-owners almost always list with the salesperson who was in contact with them most frequently in a helpful way.**

After asking questions, try to get inside the house. The following opener is simple and gets to the point. Used with the right tone of voice, it produces great results:

Salesperson: "Mr. Seller, you have a lovely house. May I see the inside of it?"

Frequently this simple question will get you in the door during your initial visit. In other instances this is where you will meet your first real resistance, usually running along lines something like this:

"My wife and I have decided we are going to sell this house ourselves. We have no intention of listing or even talking to a salesperson. Spending more time with you would serve no useful purpose."

Answer the objection this way:

Salesperson: "Mr. Seller, I understand how you feel. I know you are trying to sell your property yourself and I would in no way discourage you from doing so. I understand your motivations and wish you the best of luck in finding a buyer on your own. Please give me a moment to explain my position and what I am willing to do to help you. I am in the business of solving people's real estate problems. As part of that job, I am willing to do a number of things to help you sell your house while you are marketing it on your own, at absolutely no cost or obligation to you."

Seller: "Why would you do that?"

Salesperson: "Many people attempting to sell their houses themselves eventually decide to work with a professional in marketing their property. I'm willing to help you out while you are working on your own to earn the opportunity of explaining my marketing program to you if and when you decide you want professional help in marketing your property."

Seller: "Exactly what are you willing to do for me at no cost or obligation?"

Salesperson: "First, I will prepare a market analysis of your property. This will include information on all properties sold in your neighborhood and information on what properties are currently for sale in this area. I also will provide information on what financing is currently available and most appropriate for your particular situation.

"Second, if you find a buyer, I will recommend resource people I know who will do a good job for you and whom you will need to contact in order to close the sale of your property. These include attorneys, title companies, pest-control companies, and surveyors. I know you can pick names out of a phone book but the people I refer to you are proven professionals in their field, charge reasonable prices, and are people I personally know you can trust."

I have had many salespersons tell me I am crazy for aiding the "enemy" by providing these services. First of all, I do not consider people trying to sell their houses on their own as enemies. I view them as potential customers and referral sources. If things work out as planned, I will make a sizable fee for representing these people. These prospects and I need each other. They are potential allies, not present enemies. Second, I very much doubt that the aid I give these people will make the difference in whether or not they are successful in selling their own property. If sales came from having a handful of comparable sales on hand, all salespersons would have to do is merely bring comps to their open houses and they would all sell. And, if I do help them sell the property on their own, I will feel good about it. The help you give to the few that are successful and do complete a sale on their own is a small price to pay for all the listings you will get.

Of course offering this assistance does not guarantee you will get in the front door on your first phone call or the first time you walk up to the house and introduce yourself. In fact you may not even get into the suggested dialogue on the first contact. If you do not, it is important to leave the prospect with a positive attitude toward you. If you knocked on the door, leave a card and follow it with a handwritten thank-you note. If you used the phone for your initial contact, you can stop by the house and leave a card, with a handwritten thank-you sent through the mail.

If you did not get in the door during your initial visit or did not earn the opportunity to present a market analysis, follow up with an in-person visit within two or three days. Have a reason to stop by. If the prospect was vague about some aspect of financing, discount points, or qualifying, gather some basic information for him or her and use that as a basis for a visit. Your introduction should be:

> "Mr. Johnson, you seemed unsure about how to qualify a buyer to see if they can obtain a loan large enough to buy your house. These are some general guidelines local lenders are using for different types of loans."

Give them information on only one aspect of selling their property on each of your visits. In this way you will be able to make a number of visits and still be able to provide them with new information each time. You may have to make four or five or as many as eight or ten personal contacts before you earn the right to present a market analysis. Do not be discouraged. If the owner initially is not enthusiastic about your visits, the fact that you are providing useful information during each visit will improve the prospect's attitude toward you.

Follow up every visit with a thank-you note and every thank-you note with another visit until you get an appointment to present a market analysis. Unflagging persistence is necessary during this stage to ensure success. During your initial and subsequent visits, do not get into any type of debate with the prospects over their ability to sell their property themselves or their ability to save the commission. If you do, you will lessen your chances of obtaining the all-important market analysis appointment. These subjects should be dealt with during the presentation of your market analysis and not before. Be persistent until you earn the right to prepare and present a market analysis.

PRESENTING YOUR MARKET ANALYSIS

Your market analysis should be prepared and presented as outlined in Chapters 6 and 7. In addition to your normal presentation, you will need to counter two specific objections that you will hear when working FSBOs: (1) "There is nothing you can do for me that I can't do myself; I really don't need you" and (2) "I'm going to save the commission." We will look at how each of these can be handled.

"There is Nothing You Can Do for Me That I Can't Do Myself"

The most common seller approach when using this objection usually goes: "I can have a lawyer or title company close the sale for a couple of hundred dollars." This statement is true. What the seller does not understand is that writing the agreement and closing the sale are the easy part of any real estate transaction. Finding the buyers and getting them to pay fair market value are the hard part. These functions are essentially what we get paid for. We must get the FSBO seller to realize that brokers and salespersons control the majority of the good buyers in the marketplace.

The main prospecting tool FSBOs have is classified advertising. Many people not in the real estate business incorrectly think that most buyers for residential real estate are found through classified advertising. Salespersons understand but property owners do not realize that most buyers are not found through newspapers ads. FBSO prospects need to learn that most buyers find out about the house they eventually buy by working with a Realtor and gaining access to the efficient system brokers have developed to share market information. Until our prospects understand this, they will be unlikely to list their property with us.

Explain the fact that the vast majority of prospective buyers work with salespersons in the following way:

> "Mr. Johnson, there are a number of reasons people prefer to work with salespersons. The first is that most properties for sale are listed with salespersons, and because of that fact most good buying prospects are in frequent contact with real estate salespersons. The second is that working with a salesperson does not directly cost the buyer any out-of-pocket money. The last reason is that a salesperson does most of the hard work for a buyer."

An excellent technique is to take a blank sheet of paper and list the reasons why most good buyers work with salespersons. Some of the reasons are:

- **Qualifying** Salespersons routinely work with prospective buyers before actually showing them houses to help them determine how large a payment they qualify for and the best type of financing available for people in their particular situation.
- **Market Research** After qualifying the buyers, salespersons search for the properties currently on the market that best suit the buyers' needs and pocketbooks.
- **Showing** Salespersons arrange for appointments, drive the buying prospects to the properties, and conduct the showings.
- **Write and Negotiate the Agreement** Working with salespersons eliminates the need of the buyer in most states to hire an attorney to write the purchase agreement and negotiate directly with the seller. These are two skills that most homeowners do not possess.

- **Arrange Financing** Salespersons arrange for the right financing with the right loan officer, a difficult task for people not active in real estate on a daily basis.
- **Handle Details and Resolve Problems** Buyers do not have to cope with all the minute details and nagging problems that seem to be a part of many real estate sales.
- **Arrange for the Closing** The agencies involved or their escrow companies arrange for settlement statements and all closing details to be handled, enabling the buyer to merely show up at the closing with the money.
- **Benefit from Full Disclosure** Although in most cases all salespersons involved in a sale represent the seller, the buyer knows that full disclosure of all pertinent facts regarding the sale must be made by all the salespersons involved. This is a degree of protection a buyer does not have when purchasing directly from an owner.
- **No Cost to Buyer** All these services are provided with no out-of-pocket expense to the buyer. Of course in many if not most cases, buyers do pay for the commission through the higher selling prices normally brought when properties are sold through a salesperson.

Many agents find the following approach effective:

"Mr. Johnson, let me ask you, with all of the services we provide, why would a buyer go to an FSBO? Only one reason: to buy the house for less than it's worth. Most buyers know that if they go through a salesperson, they will end up paying market value or close to it for the real estate they buy.

"The most desirable buyers work mostly with salespersons. In fact the following categories of buyers work almost exclusively with salespersons and will not even look at properties offered by owners: first-time buyers, out-of-town buyers, and people who have sold their present property through salespersons and are moving up or down in the marketplace.

"The flip side of this coin is that most people looking at properties offered by an owner are the least desirable kind of prospects a seller can encounter. They include investors (notorious bargain-hunters), people who have attended 'buy real estate with no money down' seminars, and prospects so poorly qualified to buy property that salespersons won't work with them."

Proceed by explaining what I call the ten percent rule of investing:

> "Mr. Johnson, many people feel that an investor's first concern is to make a profit. In reality, that is an investor's second concern. Their first concern is to get their initial investment back. This is referred to as 'return of' investment. For that reason most investors will not buy a property unless they can get it for at least ten percent less than it is worth. Their reasoning is simple. That ten percent discount will pay for the majority of their selling costs when they decide to dispose of the property. If worse comes to worse and they have to sell it for what the market value was when they bought it, they will at least break even.
>
> "Buying at least ten percent below market value also means any increase in value will be all profit. This is referred to as 'return on' investment. When buying at a ten percent discount, investors will not have to wait for property values to go up to get their initial investment back. Of course this ten percent discount more than wipes out the savings incurred in not paying a commission."

Merely telling a seller going the FSBO route that his or her chances are slim has little effect. They see that as "typical salesman hype." Explain the facts. When you explain specifically how the odds are stacked against them, you will begin to deliver the message in a meaningful way.

"I'm Going to Save the Commission"

People trying to sell their own house often wrongly believe they will be able to save the whole commission. The way to approach this objection is to take another blank sheet of paper and analyze their potential savings. Use dialogue similar to:

> "Mr. Johnson, the main reason a person tries to sell his property himself is to try and save the cost of the commission. I understand how you feel. Seven percent is a lot of money and if I thought I could save that amount by selling my home myself, I would try to do it also. The only problem is that the true savings, if any, a seller ends up with is usually far less than that. Let's take a look at the potential savings in your particular situation.
>
> "Your house is worth approximately $80,000. That would make the commission and potential savings $5,600 . . . if

you could sell it for full market value and not have to pay a real estate agency for their services."

At this point, take out a blank sheet of paper and write "Potential Savings" at the top of the page. Then write "$5,600" toward the right side of the paper. Continue by saying:

"Experience in working with people trying to sell their property themselves has taught me that the first thing most potential buyers say is: 'You are not paying a commission, let's split the savings.' This reduces your potential savings by $2,800.

"The next consideration is the cost of advertising. The average time on the market for this area is 72 days (use your current local figure) before a buyer is found. If you advertise every weekend for ten weeks, you can easily spend $500. This is a cost paid for by me and my company if you decide to let us represent you in the sale. This reduces your potential savings to $2,300.

"If you are fortunate enough to find a qualified buyer, you will need to have a sales agreement prepared and have the sale closed. I hope you were not planning on using a blank form and writing up the sale yourself. The potential for a costly mistake far outweighs the potential savings. To have an attorney write the agreement and have the attorney or title company prepare and handle the closing will cost you at least $400. (Again, use a figure appropriate for your locale.) This brings the potential savings down to $1,900.

"As I mentioned earlier, the only people that shop for-sale-by-owners are investors and other bargain-hunters. Normally, investors won't buy property unless it is at least ten percent less than market value. In that case, you already lost the commission and three percent more. But say you find a relatively easy-to-work-with investor. Even in this case, most investors will not move forward on a sale at this point without a further concession on the part of the seller. They want to get a deal. I call that the 'bargain-hunter discount.' We will use a very conservative figure of $1,000. That drops the potential savings to $900.

"And, you will notice we haven't even figured a value on your time and the effort you will need to put into this transaction to resolve all the hassles and take care of the countless details that will have to be followed up in detail to get it closed.

"Relatively speaking, this is a small savings indeed when you consider how greatly the odds are stacked against people trying to sell their own property. Studies consistently show a very small rate of success among people attempting to sell their own property.

"The fact of the matter is that in most instances people who are successful in selling their own houses negotiate away the very commissions they propose to save and more."

Breaking down the desired "savings" in this manner is a good way to overcome the "I'm going to save the commission" objection. In most cases a competent salesperson will earn his or her commission or more by providing the sellers with higher net profits than they would have received by selling the property themselves. The exposure a professional salesperson can provide a property, plus the knowledge of the marketplace, financing, and his or her experience in negotiating sales agreements provides a real advantage, allowing him or her to obtain every possible dollar out of a property for the seller.

STRESS THE POSITIVES

You now need to move from the disadvantages of owners trying to sell their property themselves to the advantages of working with a professional. Again start with a blank sheet of paper and list the advantages. Follow each with an oral explanation. If you do not trust your memory, use a photocopied list. Among the advantages that can be stressed are:

- **Agents Provide a Buffer** By working with a licensed salesperson, a property owner avoids having to deal directly with prospective buyers. A salesperson is far better equipped than an owner to negotiate a sale at the best price and terms.
- **Safety** Having a property listed prevents the situation of strangers knocking on the front door wanting to see the house. When a property is listed, the owner is assured that all prospects coming through his or her house will be accompanied by a salesperson.
- **Access to Buying Prospects** Real estate salespersons have access to far more and better-qualified prospective buyers than any owner could possibly contact. (Refer above to the section, "There is nothing you can do for me that I can't do myself.")

- **Multiple-Listing Service** The MLS provides exposure unavailable to people selling their own property and opens up the sale of the property to the most desirable buying prospects currently active in the marketplace.
- **Institutional Advertising** The total of all advertising done by real estate agencies generates calls from buyers that can be channeled to the listing prospect's particular house.
- **Expertise in Financing** Accomplished salespersons have the ability to make many a seemingly impossible sale work through their knowledge of financing.
- **Savings in Selling Costs** The listing broker or listing salesperson in virtually all cases pays for all advertising costs. This provides a significant savings for the property owner.
- **Professionally Conducted Showings** Licensed salespersons know how to show a house to its best advantage. Their professional training enables them to sell the property at the top of its fair range.
- **No Missed Prospects** A prospective buyer can find a salesperson to obtain information about a listing virtually any day of the week at any time. People selling their own property frequently are not home and miss calls from prospective buyers.
- **Knowledge of the Marketplace** As a result of being full-time professionals, salespersons have a depth of knowledge of the marketplace that no private property owner has. This knowledge includes how to prepare the property for sale, promote it effectively, and negotiate an agreement to the seller's best advantage and is probably the most important advantage of listing exclusively with a salesperson.

THE ROLE OF PERSISTENCE

All of the these techniques for working with FSBO prospects have been refined in the field and proved successful time and time again. But success in working FSBOs demands more than knowing the right words to say to counter objections and win the prospect's business. The commodity most needed when working FSBOs is persistence.

Let me give you an example. I once came across an owner marketing his own home in a neighborhood adjacent to mine. It was in a desirable area and in excellent condition. In addition it had a great, low-interest assumable loan. I was determined to list that property. I was persistent and contacted the prospect on the average of every four days. I finally listed the property after six weeks. I felt pretty good as I had weathered heavy competition from other salespersons trying to obtain the listing. After putting the property on the market, I asked the seller how he happened to pick me over the seemingly dozens of others trying to list the house. I will never forget his words: "You called or stopped by every four or five days. You frequently mailed newspaper clippings and magazine articles about real estate to me. And every time, you had some useful information or selling tips for me. I figured any salesperson that helpful would do a good job in trying to get my house sold." With that example in mind, I repeat Jim Londay's Law of Working FSBOs: "Owners trying to sell their own property will most often list with the agent who has contacted them most frequently in a helpful way."

PART III

OBTAINING AND SERVICING THE LISTING

CHAPTER 6

PREPARING THE LISTING PRESENTATION

The desired result of all seller prospecting is to provide a salesperson with a list of property owners who want and need to sell their property. After a valid prospective seller is found, a salesperson is well-advised to spend whatever time is necessary to prepare a complete market analysis and listing presentation tailored to the prospective seller's situation. If you understand the marketplace and organize your material, a superb listing presentation should take no more than one to one and one-half hours to prepare—a small time investment when you consider the potential income at stake and the time involved in locating valid prospects.

A reasonable goal is to list at least 75 percent of all properties eventually placed on the market on which you have completed formal presentations. This percentage is achievable if you prepare and present your presentation correctly and follow up faithfully. If you are obtaining 50 percent or more of the listing presentations you make, you are already a top lister. You will need only minor changes and improvements in your approach to become a listing superstar. If you list less than 50 percent, you must rebuild your listing presentation to better meet the needs and expectations of your prospective sellers.

GATHERING INFORMATION

The groundwork for a great presentation is laid during the initial fact-gathering appointment. An astute salesperson will gather information not only on the property but also on the owner's motivations and concerns.

The main objective of the initial phone contact is to obtain the appointment. Keep your focus on getting the appointment. Serious fact-gathering should wait until you meet the prospect in person. Use words similar to the following when making the initial appointment:

> "Mrs. Quedensley, determining the top market value of your house and how it should be marketed requires two visits. The first will take 20 to 30 minutes. During this visit, I will take measurements of your property and gather the information I will need to prepare my analysis. During the second visit, I will present my findings to you and explain how I arrived at them."

Wait until you are face-to-face with the prospect before initiating serious fact-finding. Because you have not won the prospect's confidence yet, avoid asking probing questions during the appointment-making telephone conversation. Asking qualifying questions on the phone frequently puts the prospect on the defensive. Give the prospect a choice of times whenever possible:

> "Would 7:30 this evening or 10 tomorrow morning be best for you?"

Be persistent when setting a time for the appointment. You are not going to list the seller's property over the phone.

THE INITIAL APPOINTMENT

Making a detailed inspection of the property, asking intelligent questions, and taking extensive notes lets the sellers know you have been thorough in your considerations when you eventually give them your list of recommendations on how the property should be marketed.

I am a firm believer in involving the owner in the actual measuring of the house. After the introductions are complete and you are ready to get to work, start with something like this:

"Mrs. Quedensley, it would be helpful if you would assist me in taking measurements of the property. I would also appreciate it if, as we go through your house, you could tell me the features you like best. Knowing the benefits you've enjoyed while living in the house can help when it comes to marketing the property in its best light."

Having the seller assist you in measuring the house gives you an opportunity to ask a series of questions and learn as much as possible about your seller's situation. With such additional information, you will be able to better answer questions and counter objections during the presentation.

Take your notes on a printed or copied form that provides space for all needed information. These forms are easy to produce using your company letterhead and a data form from a blank listing agreement. They help create a good overall impression and ensure you gather all the facts you will need to complete your market analysis (*see* Example 23 for a sample Measure-Up Sheet).

Learn as much as you can about the sellers while making your tour. Their situation and motivations are as important to you as the square footage. Use a relaxed approach. Store personal information in your memory as much as possible. Your prospect would be uncomfortable if he or she were aware that you were taking written notes about their personal lives and plans. Confine your note-taking mainly to facts regarding the property with a few discreetly taken notes about the seller's personal situation. Following the initial appointment, take the first opportunity to write down all the personal information about the prospect you are carrying in your head. You will need this information later. Do not trust your memory.

During the measure-up appointment, determine if the prospects are moving out of town. If they are, try to obtain permission to give them a referral in the city to which they are moving. Inform them that you have an affiliate in the forwarding city who can contact them and send them whatever information they desire about real estate, schools, maps, and civic affairs. In the event they already have been referred to another salesperson, tell them that they could find it very helpful to receive information from more than one source.

Work hard to earn the right to send out the referral. Your purpose in this situation is not the possible referral fee. You are

Example 23

LONDAY

Real Estate Company

MEASURE-UP SHEET

NAME _____

ADDRESS _____

PHONE NUMBERS: WORK _____ HOME _____

LOAN COMPANY _____ LOAN # _____

MORTGAGE BALANCE AFTER _____ PAYMENT: _____

ESCROW BALANCE AFTER _____ PAYMENT: _____

PAYMENT P & I _____ T & I _____ TOTAL _____

TYPE _____ RATE _____ ORIG DATE _____

COMMENTS: _____

_____

_____

_____

_____

EXTERIOR DIAGRAM

# BR			# BA		$		
			RESIDENTIAL				
Ad					L #		
Style		Poss	Oc	Age	Area	Bk	
C	D	L	Room Size		SID	LB	
			LR	B%	WO	CC	
			DR	Ext	FP	1 Mtg	
			Kit	RF	HT	Mtg. Bal	
			FR	Fen	CA	Type	Int
			RR	Pav	P/H	$	T I
			BR	Swr	R/O	Tax 19	$
			BR	Wtr	Dsh	LC	WRAP
			BR	Gas	Disp	SA	CASH
			BR	BA		LA/GVT	CNV
Grd		J Hi			LA/OTH	CNV 10	
Par		Hi			VA	CNV 5	
Legal					FHA	2 FL	
		Lot Sz.			EML	FIN. B	
Remarks					LL	FSF	
B #	P		A			R	

Car Gar appears as a spanning sub-header above Room Size columns.

This information, although believed to be accurate, is not guaranteed

Suite 402, Hillcrest Landing, Omaha, NE 68127
(402) 733-5443

doing this to help you get the listing. After the appointment, get in touch with a referral salesperson through the network of which you are a member or through a directory.

If at all possible, talk directly to the salesperson who will be contacting your prospect. Explain to him or her that you have yet to land the listing and that you will be making your formal listing presentation on a specific date and time. Ask the referral salesperson to call your prospect 30 to 45 minutes before your scheduled presentation appointment. He or she can call earlier but under no circumstances should the salesperson call after the time you give your listing presentation.

Having the referral salesperson call immediately before your listing presentation will make you appear to the prospect as a person who takes care of details and gets results, a salesperson they would be confident with in listing their home. This positive first impression paves the way for your listing presentation and increases the chances of landing the listing.

Although you may not personally know the referral salesperson, he or she should be able to score some points in your favor with the prospect. Provide the referral salesperson with as much information as possible about the prospect's situation before he or she makes the telephone call to the prospect. Give the referral salesperson enough information about yourself so that he or she can feel comfortable discussing and promoting you. In many instances I have arrived at a listing presentation while the prospect was still talking on the telephone with the referral salesperson. This is a sign that he or she is doing a good job of "connecting" with your listing prospect. If the opportunity arises, get on the telephone with the salesperson and help coordinate what can be done for the prospect.

Many salespersons feel that the act of sending the referral to this person is reward enough for his or her efforts. I disagree. If a good job was done, a telephone call and a personal note of thanks are in order. In addition, add this salesperson to your personal referral network (*see* Chapter 12).

DATA RESEARCH

To prepare an effective listing presentation, you will need to gather information from a number of sources. The following information sources are used most frequently:

Multiple-listing service records

This is potentially your most valuable source for information on completed sales, pending sales, expired listings, and houses currently on the market. Virtually all multiple-listing services provide a final sold service designed for use by appraisers. Subscribe to this service if you intend to be an active lister. The appraiser's final sold service provides the most comprehensive and up-to-date source of information available in most cities (*see* the example of final sales information in the sample listing presentation that concludes this chapter).

Keep final sales data indefinitely. They provide valuable data on the history of the subject property and its neighborhood.

Appraisers

At times you will be unable to find enough comparable sales to make an informed estimate of a property's value. If you have a good working relationship with a full-time appraiser, he or she can provide you with market data that is unavailable through the MLS. Not all sales go through the MLS and most appraisers keep an up-to-date file on properties sold outside the system.

A full-time appraiser's opinion can also be helpful when estimating the market value of a unique property. Do not hesitate to seek help from someone more qualified than yourself if you are unable to make an independent, informed, and accurate market value estimate. Many appraisers will help salespersons in this way without charging a fee. Reciprocate by directing any possible appraisal business to the appraiser who helps you when you need it.

Courthouse

In most jurisdictions the courthouse is the source for legal descriptions, lot sizes, property taxes, mill levies, and special assessments. Obtain all of this information on your subject property before preparing your presentation.

Title companies

A potential seller sometimes has questions regarding the title of the property he or she is selling. This is especially true in estate or inheritance sales or when selling the property of a person legally incompetent to manage his or her own affairs. In these instances the salesperson should contact a title company as soon as possible to determine what needs to be done to convey a clear title. A salesperson who completes this task before the property is listed gains credibility. Determining what title problems a property has and how they are most easily solved will have to be done eventually. Doing it before the listing presentation will increase your chances of landing the listing.

Plat books

Many houses you try to list will be located on irregularly shaped lots or will have indefinable lot boundaries. In these cases it is helpful to make a copy of the lot as it appears in a plat book to include in your permanent file on the property and also to include in the listing presentation.

CONTENTS OF A TYPICAL LISTING PRESENTATION

Every listing presentation should be tailored to the individual prospect. Depending on the circumstances, a well-prepared presentation can run anywhere from 12 to 30 pages or more. When compiling your packet, include multiple copies of all pass-out materials. Make enough copies so that each person at the presentation will have his or her own set of the market data, estimate sheets, and proposed marketing materials that will be covered at the presentation. The presentation will flow more smoothly if the husband and wife do not have to read over each other's shoulders and you do not have to read upside down.

The following subsections are materials most often used in residential presentations. Not all are used in every presentation. Samples of each can be found in the sample presentation materials at the end of this chapter (pp. 107–125).

All materials in your presentation should be typed. Handwritten insertions look unprofessional. Be sure that the finished product is neat and clean with no typographical errors or smudges.

The Cover Sheet

The cover sheet should be typed on your company letterhead. It should include the words "Prepared for" and the property owner's name; the address, city, and state of the subject property; the date; and the name of the person preparing the report. A photo of the subject property is a nice addition that takes little time and effort.

Subject Property Data Sheet

All information collected on the subject property should be on this sheet. A photocopy of the property information section of the completed listing agreement will provide most of this information. Any items relevant to the property's value but not included on the MLS sheet should be added. This information is placed at the beginning of the packet because it will form the basis for your discussion of the property's current market value.

Computer Printout

If your MLS uses a computerized system to release market data, run a printout detailing comparable sales, pending sales, expired listings, and properties on the market. The printout will establish some basic marketing facts to the prospective seller. It informs the seller that not all houses sell during the listing period, that there is plenty of competition (similar houses on the market), and that pricing a property is not as simple a matter as it seems. This works best if the subject property is in a clearly defined subdivision. It is less effective if the property is in an older neighborhood with properties in a wide variety of styles and price ranges.

Comparable Final Solds

Comparable final solds form the basis on which you will estimate the fair range of the market value of the subject property. If possible, use a form of comparables that includes photos of the sold properties. Computer printouts of final sales data do not carry the same credibility as does an information sheet with a photo. The average owner cannot absorb and understand the confusing mass of numbers involved when comparing a large number of final sales. However, owners can and do relate to photos of houses that appear the same as theirs. With that basis established, you can discuss the differences between the two properties and the effect these differences have on market value.

Include as many relevant final sales as you can find, from a minimum of three to 15 or more. Include only properties you feel give a valid basis for comparison. If you have six good final sales within a $3,000 range and two others that sold $5,000 higher or lower than the six best, delete those not within the range. Including properties that sold for unusually high or low prices will only confuse a potential seller. You are under no obligation to give your prospect *all* available information. Include only finals that you feel provide a valid basis for consideration. You may want to have copies of the final sales you did not use with you when you do your presentation in case the prospect knows about one of these sales and asks you about it. Including all the market data you can find is a disservice to the owner, who will have enough trouble making sense of the relevant material included.

Although I use the terms "comps" and "comparables" frequently in this chapter, do not use these terms when talking to prospects. Salespersons use these terms on a daily basis and know what they mean. However, the term "comparable" has a negative connotation to many people not in the real estate business. Sellers feel there is no property "comparable" to theirs. On one level, this is true. Owners focus on what they feel are the advantages their property has over the final solds you present and not on the similarities that form the basis for comparison. For this reason refer to comps as "properties similar to yours that have recently sold in your neighborhood."

Similar Properties Currently on the Market

The purpose of including properties currently for sale similar to your seller's house is to ensure you do not overprice the house in relation to its competition. Include these in your presentation packet with caution. Property owners frequently assume that the asking price of these properties has something to do with their market value. This misconception can be difficult to dispel. (*See* Chapter 7, "Getting the Listing," for tips on coping with this problem.)

Include photocopies of all relevant properties currently for sale listed with the MLS. You may either copy entire pages and highlight the relevant properties, or you can cut the individual listings out of the book, tape them to a page, and make copies from that sheet.

Many salespersons find it helpful to drive through the entire area surrounding the prospect's house to see if there are any "For Sale by Owners" or properties for sale recently listed but not yet in the MLS book. Your prospects are sure to be aware of every property for sale in their neighborhood. Even though you may not have detailed information on every FSBO in the prospect's neighborhood, try to be aware of their presence. Make every effort to be aware of all market activity in the prospect's area.

Current Pending Sales

Using the MLS computer or printed data from the MLS, compile a list of all current pending sales similar in location and style to your prospect's property. Look up each property identified in previous MLS sold books or records. Make photocopies of the information sheet and the accompanying photograph of each pending.

After you obtain this information, find out what the individual properties sold for, the terms under which they were sold, the status of the sales, and their projected closing dates. The most important of these is the sales price. This information can be difficult to obtain at times. Your best possible sources are the listing person or salesperson of the pending properties or the closing secretary or escrow company handling the closing. Delete from your presentation any pending sales on which you are unable to obtain this information. Organize the information in a way that can be easily presented to and understood by your prospects.

Expired Listings

Compile a comprehensive list of all cancelled or expired listings in the area of the prospect's property. Using the computer or MLS records, gather as much information as you can on each property. You will not spend much time on this material during your listing presentation. Include it to show your sellers in a graphic way that not all properties sell. Include this whether market conditions are good or bad at the time of your presentation. Having this information in your packet will make it easier to get the sellers to price their property correctly.

Market Activity Summary

Virtually all multiple-listing services put out a weekly or monthly compilation of market activity that includes summaries of properties on the market and recent sales activity. The information you want to compile (or highlight, if using photocopies) should include the following facts on sales activity: number of similar properties sold for different time spans (week, month, etc.), percentage of dollar amount of average negotiation, average market time, and the percent of listed properties that expired unsold. This information will give your seller an idea of what to expect when placing the house on the market.

The summary of properties currently on the market (the seller's competition) should include the number of similar properties for sale, average asking price, and the average number of days they have been on the market unsold. This gives your sellers some perspective on the challenge they face when marketing their property. With the possible exception of the comparable solds, such information will do more to gain your seller's cooperation in pricing the property than any other portion of your presentation. It is worth the time and effort to compile the most recent data available when preparing your presentation.

Suggested Repairs Summary

In many instances, your seller will be able to net more from a sale if certain improvements to the property are made. On your company letterhead, compile a list of what you feel the seller should do to improve the chances of selling the property at the top of its fair range in the shortest period of time. Merely telling your seller that work needs to be done does not have the same impact or get the same results as leaving a typed, itemized list of items you would like completed.

In almost all cases, the seller will appreciate your frankness. Most sellers have a strong desire to do what they can to improve the marketability of their property. Getting the property in the best possible condition is one of the best areas in which a seller and salesperson can work as a team to achieve the highest net proceeds possible.

Suggested Financing Options

Financing options are a useful inclusion if marketing conditions or the seller's situation are such that you feel it would help the marketability of the property to offer alternate financing options. Determine the options you would like the seller to offer. Include examples of how these options work. Keep it simple but include enough to be able to explain how the options apply to your seller's situation. Your sellers will be exposed to the idea of using these options even if they initially are unwilling to do so. This is part of educating your sellers so that they will be knowledgeable enough to take corrective steps if the property does not sell in a timely fashion.

Seller's Estimate Sheet

This can be in the form of a settlement statement or an itemized, fill-in-the-blank form. Use whichever format you prefer.

Discount Point Explanation Sheet

Make copies of the "discount point explanation sheet" on your letterhead and include it in every listing presentation in which you wish the seller to offer FHA and VA terms.

Company Promotional Material

Keep this portion of your presentation brief. Few people are interested in hearing you talk at great lengths about the superiority of your agency. All promotional material used should relate to the benefits the seller will receive when listing with your company.

Start with a brief summary of your company's history. Include statistics you believe add to the stature of your company, such as market share, sales volume, and number of salespersons. Mention related services your agency provides: referral network, guaranteed sales programs, appraisal services, and other benefits. Prospects tire quickly when listening to self-serving boasts of how great your company is. Spend the minimum time necessary to make the points you think are the legitimate advantages of listing with your company.

Personal Promotional Material

Keep this to a minimum: no longer than one page. Do not include photocopies of your real estate license (everyone already knows you have it), 8″ x 10″ glossy photos of yourself (you are right in front of them), or photocopies of your "million dollar club" certificates. These things will not help if the rest of your presentation does not establish you as a professional. I am not saying that you should avoid selling yourself. Demonstrating your knowledge of the marketplace and outlining what you can do for the prospect are the best way of promoting yourself. If you are good, you do not have to say it.

Sample "Open House" Brochures

Provide copies (one for each person at the presentation) of "Just Listed," "Open House," and "Just Sold" brochures for every property on which you have previously mailed promotions in the prospects' area of town. Include brochures of all properties you have sold in the prospects' marketing area. If during the past three years you have listed 20 properties within two miles of the prospects' house, include samples of each. They demonstrate to your prospects that you know how to sell houses in the area in which they live and will do more to establish your ability and experience than all the awards, plaques, and certificates a salesperson could earn in a lifetime.

Sample "Salesperson" Brochures

These are similar in appearance to "Open House" brochures but are designed to be distributed to real estate salespersons. They differ in that they contain all listing information normally found in a multiple-listing book. Also included is any promotional blurb the listing salesperson feels would stimulate interest from other salespersons. (*See* Chapter 8, "Obtaining Price, Terms, and Condition Adjustments," for a full explanation of their use.) As with the "Open House" brochures, include as many examples of these promotional brochures as you have in your sample file.

Samples of Other Regularly Used Advertising

These should consist of examples of all other types of advertising you actually will use to promote the prospects' property if they list with you. Introduce the subject of institutional advertising orally if you want to make it a part of your presentation.

"As I'm sure you've seen by our television advertising, we sell the most houses of any agency in the city."

If the advertising has been effective, it will have said everything that needs to be said. A brief reference to it will get the maximum good out of it.

"Thanks for Showing My Listing" Form

This form demonstrates how you plan to monitor marketplace feedback.

Proposed Marketing Schedule

This will be used as a trial close as outlined in the next chapter.

Listing Agreement

The listing agreement will be your final insertion. Make sure it is completely filled out except for the price and possession blanks. Have the necessary number of copies stapled together with carbons inserted.

ASSEMBLING THE MATERIAL

Being organized is the key to consistently preparing a professional presentation. Keep a separate section of a file drawer or cabinet for the materials used in your listing presentations. This simple step saves an enormous amount of time. Include file folders with ample supplies of all materials or forms you regularly use in your presentations.

When assembling your final presentation, compile all inserts in the order in which they appear in this chapter and place them in a pocket report cover. Tape or glue a business card to the inside of the report cover. Using an unbound pocket folder allows you to tailor each presentation to the prospect's situation. Include all materials you think apply to the situation of the property owner you will be seeing.

You will use all 20 inserts in one listing presentation in only a few instances. What to include and what to delete with different prospects can only be learned by trial and error. If you are not sure whether to include an item, it is best to make it a part of the presentation.

APPENDIX: SAMPLE PRESENTATION MATERIALS

LISTING PRESENTATION CONTENTS CHECKLIST

- ☐ COVER SHEET
- ☐ SUBJECT PROPERTY DATA SHEET
- ☐ COMPUTER PRINTOUT
- ☐ COMPARABLE FINAL SOLDS
- ☐ CURRENT PENDING SALES
- ☐ CURRENT "ON MARKETS"
- ☐ EXPIRED LISTINGS
- ☐ MARKET ACTIVITY SUMMARY
- ☐ SUGGESTED REPAIRS SUMMARY
- ☐ SUGGESTED FINANCING OPTIONS
- ☐ SELLER'S ESTIMATED NET SHEET
- ☐ DISCOUNT POINT EXPLANATION SHEET
- ☐ COMPANY PROMOTIONAL MATERIAL*
- ☐ PERSONAL PROMOTIONAL MATERIAL*
- ☐ SAMPLE "OPEN" BROCHURES
- ☐ SAMPLE "SALESPERSON" BROCHURES
- ☐ SAMPLES OF OTHER REGULARLY USED ADVERTISING*
- ☐ "THANKS FOR SHOWING MY LISTING" FORM
- ☐ PROPOSED MARKETING SCHEDULE
- ☐ LISTING AGREEMENT

*Samples of these not included. Use the material provided by your company.

LONDAY
Real Estate Company

PREPARED FOR:

MR. AND MRS. ROBERT THORNTON

FOR PROPERTY LOCATED AT:

1446 DIVISION

JUNE 28, 19__

BY:

JAMES K. LONDAY
ASSOCIATE BROKER

Suite 402, Hillcrest Landing, Omaha, NE 68127
(402) 733-5443

LONDAY
Real Estate Company

SUBJECT PROPERTY DATA SHEET

ADDRESS: _____

LEGAL DESCRIPTION _____

STYLE _____

EXTERIOR MAIL LEVEL SQUARE FOOTAGE _____

SECOND STORY SQUARE FOOTAGE _____

FINISHED BASEMENT SQUARE FOOTAGE _____

BEDROOMS _____   BATHS _____

DINING ROOM _____   FAMILY ROOM _____

FIREPLACE _____   HEATING _____

AIR CONDITIONING _____   POWER HUMIDIFIER _____

RANGE/OVEN _____   DISHWASHER _____

TYPE OF CURRENT FINANCING _____

ASSUMABLE? _____   CURRENT BALANCE _____

PAYMENT _____   INCLUDES _____

ADDITIONAL COMMENTS _____

_____

_____

_____

_____

_____

Suite 402, Hillcrest Landing, Omaha, NE 68127
(402) 733-5443

COMPUTER PRINTOUT

LAKE COUNTY
PROFILE SALES ACTIVITY
RESIDENTIAL PROPERTIES FOR JULY 1985 - DECEMBER 1985

THIS TABLE SHOWS A MARKET ANALYSIS OF EACH SECTION OF THIS SERVICE AND COMPARES EACH SECTION IN RELATION TO THE OVERALL ACTIVITY.

ZIP	UNIT SALES	% TOTAL MARKET	DOLLAR VOLUME	% SALES ACTIVITY	AVERAGE LISTING PRICE	AVERAGE SELLING PRICE	% OF LISTING PRICE RECEIVED	MEDIAN SALE PRICE*	AVERAGE SALE TIME-HOUSES SOLD	AVERAGE LISTING PRICE HOUSES NOT SOLD
ALL	2392	100.00	182,420,942	54.32	79,654	76,262	95.74	66,000	82.73	90,234
60002	135	5.64	9,957,912	52.48	78,395	73,762	94.08	65,000	109.71	86,986
60015	2	.08	245,000	37.50	124,400	122,500	98.47	122,500	12.50	128,180
60020	47	1.96	2,437,150	35.26	57,204	51,854	90.64	52,000	141.68	57,421
60030	105	4.38	8,897,830	54.83	88,204	84,741	96.07	76,000	69.73	98,253
60031	115	4.80	9,288,375	49.66	84,522	80,768	95.55	73,000	85.65	93,254
60041	48	2.00	3,046,690	44.82	67,961	63,472	93.39	54,250	143.70	91,076
60042	38	1.58	2,179,200	59.34	59,626	57,347	96.17	59,200	82.97	78,118
60044	29	1.21	3,610,850	67.30	132,813	124,512	93.74	125,000	103.06	129,729
60045	6	.25	1,125,500	60.00	205,316	187,583	91.36	140,000	86.50	316,816
60046	182	7.60	13,863,740	53.52	79,156	76,174	96.23	74,250	67.37	93,308
60047	95	3.97	9,877,541	55.65	108,256	103,974	96.04	92,500	64.47	169,505
60048	183	7.65	25,113,940	67.67	143,031	137,234	95.94	135,900	70.81	164,918
60050	76	3.17	5,266,283	44.81	72,453	69,293	95.63	63,750	91.92	94,112
60060	182	7.60	15,170,785	64.60	86,174	83,355	96.72	76,500	67.21	116,740
60061	168	7.02	12,630,806	63.52	77,766	75,183	96.67	66,750	75.43	74,105
60064	30	1.25	1,423,100	43.92	49,713	47,436	95.42	45,000	92.26	51,270
60069	1	.04	91,500	60.00	94,900	91,500	96.41	91,500	100.00	91,200
60073	195	8.15	9,529,336	55.49	50,879	48,868	96.04	47,700	79.24	53,924
60075	1	.04	80,000	50.00	84,900	80,000	94.22	80,000	26.00	259,000
60081	24	1.00	1,428,350	35.63	62,954	59,514	94.53	50,375	141.04	85,941
60083	8	.33	838,900	32.43	109,512	104,862	95.75	107,750	108.25	158,500
60084	53	2.21	3,734,785	53.84	73,573	70,467	95.77	64,500	89.94	119,213
60085	238	9.94	13,646,800	58.24	59,683	57,339	96.07	53,700	73.15	60,190
60087	175	7.31	10,951,675	61.65	65,087	62,581	96.14	60,000	78.88	77,511
60089	7	.29	783,500	81.81	115,557	111,928	96.85	118,500	27.14	102,700
60090	4	.16	464,500	62.50	120,550	116,125	96.32	125,750	71.25	101,933
60096	52	2.17	3,564,700	57.69	71,037	68,551	96.50	68,100	85.71	80,925
60099	148	6.18	8,960,194	49.03	63,084	60,541	95.96	56,500	92.02	67,106
60999	45	1.88	4,212,000	34.09	100,055	93,600	93.54	83,000	118.13	123,560

* THE MEDIAN SALE PRICE HAS AS MANY LISTINGS ABOVE IT AS BELOW IT.

Reprinted with permission of the Lake County Board of REALTORS®, Lake Villa, IL.

COMPARABLE FINAL SOLDS

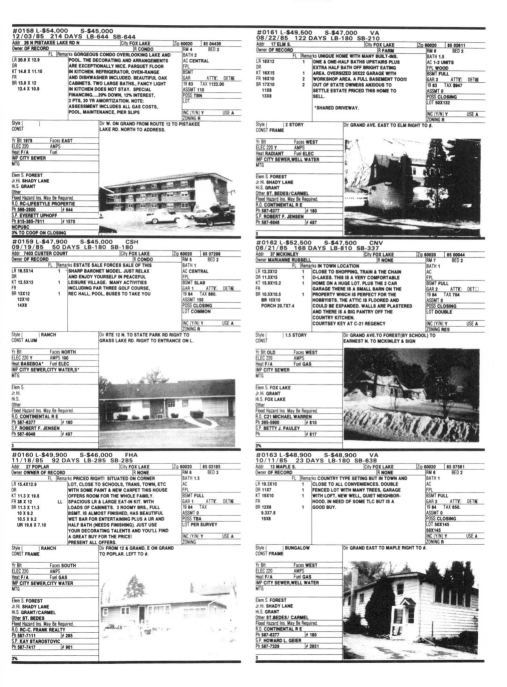

#0158 L-$54,000   S-$45,000
12/03/85 214 DAYS LB-644 SB-644

Addr 26 N PISTAKEE LAKE RD N	City FOX LAKE	Zip 60020	85 04436
Owner OF RECORD	R CONDO	RM 4	BED 2

FL Remarks GORGEOUS CONDO OVERLOOKING LAKE AND POOL. THE DECORATING AND ARRANGEMENTS ARE EXCEPTIONALLY NICE. PARQUET FLOOR IN KITCHEN. REFRIGERATOR, OVEN-RANGE AND DISHWASHER INCLUDED. BEAUTIFUL OAK CABINETS. TWO LARGE BATHS, FANCY LIGHT IN KITCHEN DOES NOT STAY. SPECIAL FINANCING.....20% DOWN, 12% INTEREST, 2 PTS, 20 YR AMORTIZATION. NOTE: ASSESSMENT INCLUDES ALL GAS COSTS, POOL, MAINTENANCE, PIER SLIPS

LR 20.9 X 12.9
DR
KT 14.8 X 11.10
FR
BR 13.8 X 12
   12.4 X 10.9

BATH 2
AC CENTRAL
FPL
BSMT
GAR   ATTY   DET N
19 83   TAX 1122.00
ASSMT 110
POSS TBN
LOT
INC [Y/N] Y   USE A
ZONING R

Style [ ]
CONST
Dir W. ON GRAND FROM ROUTE 12 TO PISTAKEE LAKE RD. NORTH TO ADDRESS.

Yr Blt 1978   Faces EAST
ELEC 220   AMPS
Heat F/A   Fuel
IMP CITY SEWER
MTG

Elem S. FOREST
Jr.Hi. SHADY LANE
Hi.S. GRANT
Other
Flood Hazard Ins. May Be Required.
R.O. RC-LIFESTYLE PROPERTIE
Ph 566-2800   # 544
S.P. EVERETT UPHOFF
Ph 815-385-7911   # 1570
NCPUBC
3% TO COOP ON CLOSING

#0161 L-$49,500   S-$47,000   VA
08/22/85 122 DAYS LB-180 SB-210

Addr 17 ELM S.	City FOX LAKE	Zip 60020	85 02611
Owner OF RECORD	R FARM	RM 8	BED 2

FL Remarks UNIQUE HOME WITH MANY BUILT-INS. ONE & ONE-HALF BATHS UPSTAIRS PLUS EXTRA HALF BATH OFF BRIGHT EATING AREA. OVERSIZED 30X22 GARAGE WITH WORKSHOP AREA. A FULL BASEMENT TOO!!! OUT OF STATE OWNERS ANXIOUS TO SETTLE ESTATE PRICED THIS HOME TO SELL.

*SHARED DRIVEWAY.

LR 18X12   1
DR
KT 16X15   1
FR 16X10   2
BR 17X10   2
   11X8
   13X8

BATH 1.5
AC 1-2 UNITS
FPL WOOD
BSMT FULL
GAR 3   ATTY   DET N
19 83   TAX $947
ASSMT 0
POSS CLOSING
LOT 50X132
INC [Y/N] Y   USE A
ZONING R

Style [ ] 2 STORY
CONST FRAME
Dir GRAND AVE. EAST TO ELM RIGHT TO #.

Yr Blt   Faces WEST
ELEC 220 Y   AMPS
Heat RADIANT   Fuel ELEC
IMP CITY SEWER, WELL WATER
MTG

Elem S. FOREST
Jr.Hi. SHADY LANE
Hi.S. GRANT
Other ST. BEDES/CARMEL
Flood Hazard Ins. May Be Required.
R.O. CONTINENTAL R E
Ph 587-6377   # 180
S.P. ROBERT F. JENSEN
Ph 587-6046   # 497
3

#0159 L-$47,900   S-$45,000   CSH
09/19/85 50 DAYS LB-180 SB-180

Addr 7403 CUSTER COURT	City FOX LAKE	Zip 60020	85 07298
Owner OF RECORD	R NONE	RM 5	BED 2

FL Remarks ESTATE SALE FORCES SALE OF THIS SHARP BARONET MODEL. JUST RELAX AND ENJOY YOURSELF IN PEACEFUL LEISURE VILLAGE. MANY ACTIVITIES INCLUDING PAR THREE GOLF COURSE, REC HALL, POOL, BUSES TO TAKE YOU

LR 16.5X14   1
DR
KT 12.5X12   1
FR
BR 13X12   1
   12X10
   14X6

BATH 1
AC CENTRAL
FPL
BSMT SLAB
GAR 1   ATTY   DET N
19 84   TAX 880.
ASSMT 150
POSS CLOSING
LOT COMMON
INC [Y/N] Y   USE A
ZONING R

Style [ ] RANCH
CONST ALUM
Dir RTE 12 N. TO STATE PARK RD RIGHT TO GRASS LAKE RD. RIGHT TO ENTRANCE ON L.

Yr Blt   Faces NORTH
ELEC 220 Y   AMPS 100
Heat BASEBOA*   Fuel ELEC
IMP CITY SEWER, CITY WATER, S*
MTG

Elem S.
Jr.Hi.
Hi.S.
Other
Flood Hazard Ins. May Be Required.
R.O. CONTINENTAL R E
Ph 587-6377   # 180
S.P. ROBERT F. JENSEN
Ph 587-6046   # 497
3

#0162 L-$52,500   S-$47,500   CNV
08/21/85 168 DAYS LB-810 SB-337

Addr 37 MCKINLEY	City FOX LAKE	Zip 60020	85 00044
Owner MARIANNE RUSSELL	R NONE	RM 7	BED 2

FL Remarks IN TOWN LOCATION CLOSE TO SHOPPING, TRAIN & THE CHAIN O-LAKES. THIS IS A VERY COMFORTABLE HOME ON A HUGE LOT. PLUS THE 2 CAR GARAGE THERE IS A SMALL BARN ON THE PROPERTY WHICH IS PERFECT FOR THE HOBBYISTS. THE ATTIC IS FLOORED AND COULD BE EXPANDED. WALLS ARE PLASTERED AND THERE IS A BIG PANTRY OFF THE COUNTRY KITCHEN.
COURTSEY KEY AT C-21 REGENCY

LR 13.3X12   1
DR 11.5X15   1
KT 15.9X15.2   1
FR
BR 10.5X10.5   1
   BR 10X10
   PORCH 20.7X7.4

BATH 1
AC
FPL
BSMT FULL
GAR 1   ATTY   DET □
19 84   TAX 704
ASSMT 0
POSS CLOSING
LOT DOUBLE
INC [Y/N] Y   USE A
ZONING RES

Style [ ] 1.5 STORY
CONST
Dir GRAND AVE.TO FOREST(BY SCHOOL) TO EARNEST N. TO MCKINLEY & SIGN

Yr Blt OLD   Faces WEST
ELEC 220   AMPS
Heat F/A   Fuel GAS
IMP CITY SEWER
MTG

Elem S. FOX LAKE
Jr.Hi. GRANT
Hi.S. FOX LAKE
Other
Flood Hazard Ins. May Be Required.
R.O. C21 MICHAEL WARREN
Ph 395-5900   # 810
S.P. BETTY J. PAULEY
Ph .   # 817
3%

#0160 L-$49,900   S-$46,000   FHA
11/18/85 92 DAYS LB-285 SB-285

Addr 27 POPLAR	City FOX LAKE	Zip 60020	85 03185
Owner OWNER OF RECORD	R NONE	RM 6	BED 3

FL Remarks PRICED RIGHT! SITUATED ON CORNER LOT, CLOSE TO SCHOOLS, TRANS, TOWN, ETC WITH SOME PAINT & NEW CARPET THIS HOUSE OFFERS ROOM FOR THE WHOLE FAMILY. SPACIOUS LR & LARGE EAT-IN KIT. WITH LOADS OF CABINETS. 3 ROOMY BRS., FULL BSMT. IS ALMOST FINISHED, HAS BEAUTIFUL WET BAR FOR ENTERTAINING PLUS A UR AND HALF BATH (NEEDS FINISHING). JUST USE YOUR DECORATING TALENTS AND YOU'LL FIND A GREAT BUY FOR THE PRICE! PRESENT ALL OFFERS.

LR 15.4X12.9
DR
KT 11.3 X 13.6
FR 38 X 12   LL
BR 11.3 X 11.3
   10 X 9.2
   10.5 X 9.2
   UR 19.6 X 7.10

BATH 1.5
AC
FPL
BSMT FULL
GAR 1   ATTY   DET N
19 84   TAX
ASSMT 0
POSS TBA
LOT PER SURVEY
INC [Y/N] Y   USE A
ZONING

Style [ ] RANCH
CONST FRAME
Dir FROM 12 & GRAND, E ON GRAND TO POPLAR. LEFT TO #.

Yr Blt   Faces SOUTH
ELEC 220   AMPS
Heat F/A   Fuel GAS
IMP CITY SEWER, CITY WATER
MTG

Elem S. FOREST
Jr.Hi. SHADY LANE
Hi.S. GRANT/CARMEL
Other ST. BEDES
Flood Hazard Ins. May Be Required.
R.O. RC-C. FRANK REALTY
Ph 587-7111   # 285
S.P. KAY STAROSTOVIC
Ph 587-7417   # 901
3%

#0163 L-$48,900   S-$48,900   VA
10/11/85 23 DAYS LB-180 SB-638

Addr 13 MAPLE S.	City FOX LAKE	Zip 60020	85 07581
Owner OF RECORD	R NONE	RM 6	BED 2

FL Remarks COUNTRY TYPE SETING BUT IN TOWN AND CLOSE TO ALL CONVENIENCES. DOUBLE FENCED LOT WITH MANY TREES, GARAGE WITH LOFT, NEW WELL, QUIET NEIGHBOR-HOOD. IN NEED OF SOME TLC BUT IS A GOOD BUY.

LR 19.3X10   1
DR 11X7   1
KT 19X10   1
FR
BR 12X8   1
   9.3X7.6
   19X8

BATH 1.5
AC
FPL
BSMT FULL
GAR 2   ATTY   DET N
19 84   TAX 650.
ASSMT 0
POSS CLOSING
LOT 50X145
   50X145
INC [Y/N] Y   USE A
ZONING R

Style [ ] BUNGALOW
CONST FRAME
Dir GRAND EAST TO MAPLE RIGHT TO #.

Yr Blt   Faces WEST
ELEC 220   AMPS
Heat F/A   Fuel GAS
IMP CITY SEWER, WELL WATER
MTG

Elem S. FOREST
Jr.Hi. SHADY LANE
Hi.S. GRANT
Other ST.BEDES/ CARMEL
Flood Hazard Ins. May Be Required.
R.O. CONTINENTAL R E
Ph 587-6377   # 180
S.P. HOWARD L. GEIER
Ph 587-7329   # 2851
3

CURRENT PENDING SALES

#01254 — FHA ASSUMPTION — $39,000

Addr **608 COLUMBUS**	Map **0** — City **MCHENRY** — Zip **60050** — **85 11008**
Owner **OF RECORD**	R

	FL	C	W	Remarks **LOOKING FOR A STARTER HOME?**	RM **5** — BED **3**
LR 15.1X10.6				**FIRST-TIME BUYERS CAN NOW AFFORD THIS**	BATH **1**
DR				**EXTREMELY WELL-BUILT HOME THAT BOASTS**	AC
KT 10.6X10				**PLASTER WALLS,NEW SIDING,3 BDRMS,1,BTH,**	FPL **WOOD**
FR				**&BRAND NEW SEPTIC.LIKE THE OLD LADY**	BSMT **SLAB**
BR 11.3X10.2				**WHO LIVED IN A SHOE,THE CURRENT OWNER**	GAR ATTN DETN
10.1X9.7				**JUST PLAIN OUT GREW IT.VERY MOTIVATED**	19 **84** TAX **324**
10.2X7.10				**SELLERS,ONE BLOCK FROM STATE PARK**	ASSMT **0**
				FHA ASSUMABLE-10%-APP.BAL.31,500	POSS **TBA**
				EXCLUDE: REFRIG,NEGO. WASHER/DRYER	LOT **60X150**
					INC [Y/N] USE **A**
					ZONING **B-1**

Style [**R**] **RANCH**	Dir **RT.12 & 120 N TO LILY LK. RD.,S 3/4 MI.**
CONST **FRAME**	**LEFT ON COLUMBUS TO #**

Yr Blt — Faces **SOUTH**	
ELEC 220 — AMPS	
Heat **BASEBOA*** — Fuel	
IMP	
Mortgage **22000** — PITI	
ASM% **10%** — Lender	
Elem S. **HILL TOP**	
Jr.Hi. **PARKLANE**	
Hi.S. **MCHENRY EAST**	
Other **MONTENI**	
Flood Hazard Ins. May Be Required.	
R.O. **COLDWELL BANKER**	
Ph **367-4700** — # **154**	
S.P. **COLLEEN E. FLEMING**	
Ph **623-4742** — # **1568**	

3%

Pending Sales Price $38,000
Conventional Financing

#01255 — $39,000

Addr **5007 WESTERN AVE**	Map **0** — City **BURTONS BR** — Zip **60050** — **86 02859**
Owner **FIRST NATIONAL BK OF CRYSTAL LAKE**	**R RESIDENTIAL**

	FL	C	W	Remarks **HANDYMAN SPECIAL ON DOUBLE LOT**	RM **6** — BED **3**
LR 21.9X11.9	1			**HAS GREAT POTENTIAL IN AREA OF NICER**	BATH **1**
DR				**HOMES.BANK WILL OFFER 15 YEAR FIXED AT**	AC
KT 13.9X7.6	1			**9.50% 3 POINTS ON 30 THOUSAND$ MORTAGE**	FPL **LIV RM**
FR				**A MUST TO SEE IF YOUR HANDY!!!**	BSMT **CRAWL**
BR 12.7X9.9	1				GAR ATTN DETN
2BR 17.1X11.9	1				19 TAX **84-688**
3BR 15.6X9.1	1				ASSMT **0**
15.3 X 7.6	1				POSS **IMMEDIATE**
UTIL 9X7.6	1				LOT
					INC [Y/N] **N** USE
					ZONING **RES**

Style [**R**] **RANCH**	Dir **176 W TO NISH ,FIRST ST WRIGHT R TILL**
CONST	**HILINE R TO WESTERN AVE R TO SIGN**

Yr Blt **999** — Faces	
ELEC 220 — AMPS	
Heat — Fuel **GAS**	
IMP **SEPTIC**	
Mortgage — PITI	
ASM% — Lender	
Elem S. **DIST.15**	
Jr.Hi. **15**	
Hi.S. **156**	
Other	
Flood Hazard Ins. May Be Required.	
R.O. **MCKEE REAL ESTATE, INC**	
Ph **541-1000** — # **523**	
S.P. **VIRGINIA MC KEE**	
Ph **541-1000** — # **2615**	

3%

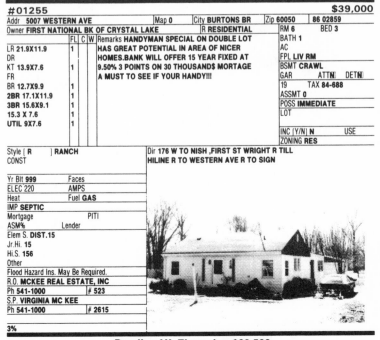

Pending VA Financing $38,500

SAMPLE "ON MARKETS"

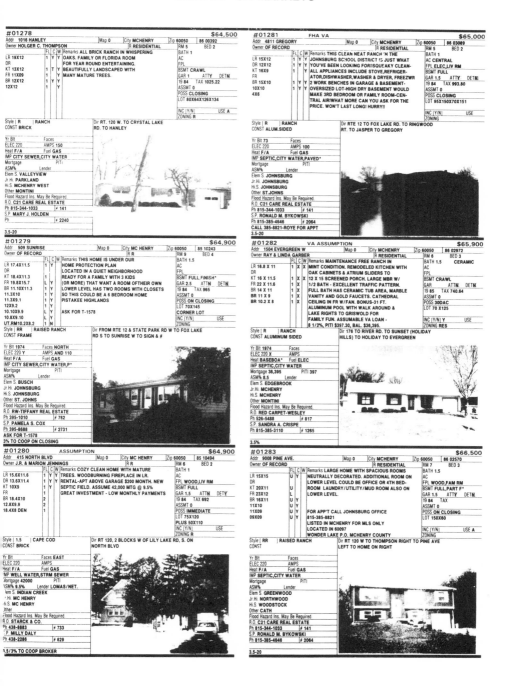

#01278 $64,500

| Addr 1016 HANLEY | Map 0 | City MCHENRY | Zip 60050 | 86 00392 |
| Owner HOLGER C. THOMPSON | | R RESIDENTIAL | RM 5 | BED 2 |

	F	L	C	W	Remarks ALL BRICK RANCH IN WHISPERING
LR 19X12	1	Y	Y		OAKS. FAMILY OR FLORIDA ROOM
DR					FOR YEAR ROUND ENTERTAINING.
KT 13X12	1	T	Y		BEAUTIFULLY LANDSCAPED WITH
FR 11X09			Y		MANY MATURE TREES.
BR 12X12	1	Y	Y		
12X12	1		Y		

BATH 1
FPL
BSMT CRAWL
GAR 1   ATTY   DETN
19 84   TAX 1025.22
ASSMT 0
POSS CLOSING
LOT 80X64X126X134
INC (Y/N)   USE A
ZONING R

Style | R | RANCH
CONST BRICK

Dir RT. 120 W. TO CRYSTAL LAKE RD. TO HANLEY

Yr Blt   Faces
ELEC 220   AMPS 150
Heat F/A   Fuel GAS
IMP CITY SEWER,CITY WATER
Mortgage   PITI
ASM%   Lender
Elem S. VALLEYVIEW
Jr. Hi. PARKLAND
H.S. MCHENRY WEST
Other MONTINI
Flood Hazard Ins. May Be Required.
R.O. C21 CARE REAL ESTATE
Ph 815-344-1033   # 141
S.P. MARY J. HOLDEN
Ph   # 2240

3.5-20

#01279 $64,900

| Addr 509 SUNRISE | Map 0 | City MC HENRY | Zip 60050 | 85 10243 |
| Owner OF RECORD | | R R | RM 9 | BED 4 |

	F	L	C	W	Remarks THIS HOME IS UNDER OUR
LR 17.4X11.5	1		Y		HOME PROTECTION PLAN
DR					LOCATED IN A QUIET NEIGHBORHOOD
KT 18.4X11.3	1		Y		READY FOR A FAMILY WITH 3 KIDS
FR 19.8X15.7	L	Y			(OR MORE) THAT WANT A ROOM OFTHEIR OWN
BR 11.10X11.3	1		Y		LOWER LEVEL HAS TWO ROOMS WITH CLOSETS
11.3X10	1		Y		SO THIS COULD BE A 6 BEDROOM HOME
11.3X9.1	1		Y		PISTAKEE HIGHLANDS
12X9.2	1		Y		
10.10X9.9	1		Y		ASK FOR T-1578
10.8X9.10	L		Y		
UT.RM10.2X8.2	1	N			

BATH 1.5
FPL
BSMT FULL.FINISH*
GAR 2.5   ATTN   DETN
19 84   TAX 965
ASSMT 0
POSS ON CLOSING
LOT 70X145
CORNER LOT
INC (Y/N)   USE
ZONING

Style | RR | RAISED RANCH
CONST FRAME

Dir FROM RTE 12 & STATE PARK RD W TO FOX LAKE RD S TO SUNRISE W TO SIGN & #

Yr Blt 1974   Faces NORTH
ELEC 220 Y   AMPS AND 110
Heat F/A   Fuel GAS
IMP CITY SEWER,CITY WATER,P*
Mortgage   PITI
ASM%   Lender
Elem S. BUSCH
Jr. Hi. JOHNSBURG
H.S. JOHNSBURG
Other ST. JOHNS
Flood Hazard Ins. May Be Required.
R.O. RW-TIFFANY REAL ESTATE
Ph 395-1010   # 762
S.P. PAMELA S. COX
Ph 395-8688   # 2731
ASK FOR T-1578
3% TO COOP ON CLOSING

#01280   ASSUMPTION $64,900

| Addr 415 NORTH BLVD | Map 0 | City MC HENRY | Zip 60050 | 85 10494 |
| Owner J.R. & MARION JENNINGS | | R R | RM 6 | BED 2 |

	F	L	C	W	Remarks COZY CLEAN HOME WITH MATURE
LR 15.6X11.6	1	Y	Y		TREES. WOODBURNING FIREPLACE IN LR.
DR 13.6X11.4	1	Y	Y		RENTAL-APT ABOVE GARAGE $200 MONTH. NEW
KT 10X9	1	Y			SEPTIC FIELD. ASSUME 42,000 MTG @ 9.5%
FR					GREAT INVESTMENT - LOW MONTHLY PAYMENTS
BR 18.4X10	2				
12.8X9.9	2				
18.4X8 DEN	2				

BATH 1
FPL WOOD,LIV RM
BSMT FULL
GAR 1.5   ATTN   DETY
19 84   TAX 692
ASSMT 0
POSS IMMEDIATE
LOT 75X120
PLUS 50X110
INC (Y/N)   USE
ZONING R

Style | 1.5 | CAPE COD
CONST BRICK

Dir RT 120, 2 BLOCKS W OF LILY LAKE RD. S. ON NORTH BLVD

Yr Blt   Faces EAST
ELEC 220   AMPS
Heat F/A   Fuel GAS
IMP WELL WATER,STRM SEWER
Mortgage 42000   PITI
ASM% 9.5%   Lender LOMAS/NET.
Elem S. INDIAN CREEK
Jr. Hi. MC HENRY
H.S. MC HENRY
Other
Flood Hazard Ins. May Be Required.
R.O. STARCK & CO.
Ph 438-8883   # 733
S.P. MILLY DALY
Ph 438-2286   # 629

3.5/3% TO COOP BROKER

#01281   FHA VA $65,000

| Addr 4811 GREGORY | Map 0 | City MCHENRY | Zip 60050 | 86 03089 |
| Owner OF RECORD | | R RESIDENTIAL | RM 5 | BED 2 |

	F	L	C	W	Remarks THIS CLEAN NEAT RANCH 'N THE
LR 15X12	1	Y	Y		JOHNSBURG SCHOOL DISTRICT IS JUST WHAT
DR 12X12	1	Y	Y		YOU'VE BEEN LOOKING FORISQUEAKY CLEAN-
KT 16X9	1		Y		ALL APPLIANCES INCLUDE STOVE,REFRIGER-
FR					ATOR,DISHWASHER,WASHER & DRYER, FREEZWR
BR 15X10	1	Y	Y		2 WORK BENCHES IN GARAGE & BASEMENT-
10X10	1	Y	Y		OVERSIZED LOT-HIGH DRY BASEMENT WOULD
4X6					MAKE 3RD BEDROOM OR FAMILY ROOM-CEN-
					TRAL AIR!WHAT MORE CAN YOU ASK FOR THE
					PRICE. WON'T LAST LONG! HURRY!!

BATH 1
AC CENTRAL
FPL ELEC,LIV RM
BSMT FULL
GAR 1.5   ATTY   DETN
19 84   TAX 993.80
ASSMT 0
POSS CLOSING
LOT 95X150X70X151
INC (Y/N)   USE
ZONING

Style | R | RANCH
CONST ALUM.SIDED

Dir RTE 12 TO FOX LAKE RD. TO RINGWOOD RT. TO JASPER TO GREGORY

Yr Blt 73   Faces
ELEC 220   AMPS 100
Heat F/A   Fuel GAS
IMP SEPTIC,CITY WATER,PAVED*
Mortgage   PITI
ASM%   Lender
Elem S JOHNSBURG
Jr. Hi. JOHNSBURG
H.S. JOHNSBURG
Other ST. JOHNS
Flood Hazard Ins. May Be Required.
R.O. C21 CARE REAL ESTATE
Ph 815-344-1033   # 141
S.P. RONALD M. BYKOWSKI
Ph 815-385-4646   # 2064
CALL 385-5821-ROYE FOR APPT
3.5-20

#01282   VA ASSUMPTION $65,900

| Addr 1504 EVERGREEN W | Map 0 | City MCHENRY | Zip 60050 | 86 02972 |
| Owner RAY & LINDA GARBER | | R RESIDENTIAL | RM 6 | BED 3 |

	F	L	C	W	Remarks MAINTENANCE FREE RANCH IN
LR 16.8 X 11	1	X	X		MINT CONDITION. REMODELED KITCHEN WITH
DR			X		OAK CABINETS & ATRIUM SLIDERS TO
KT 16 X 11.5	1	X	X		12 X 15 SCREENED PORCH. LARGE MBR W/
FR 22 X 11.6	1		X		1/2 BATH - EXCELLENT TRAFFIC PATTERN.
BR 14 X 11	1		X		FULL BATH HAS CERAMIC TUB AREA, MARBLE
BR 11 X 9	1		X		VANITY AND GOLD FAUCETS. CATHEDRAL
BR 10.2 X 8	1		X		CEILING IN FR W/FAN. BONUS-31 FT.
					ALUMINUM POOL WITH WALK AROUND &
					LAKE RIGHTS TO GRISWOLD FOR
					FAMILY FUN. ASSUMABLE VA LOAN -
					8 1/2%, PITI $397.30, BAL. $38,395.

BATH 1.5   CERAMIC
AC
FPL
BSMT CRAWL
GAR   ATTN   DETN
19 84   TAX 740.64
ASSMT 0
POSS 30DAC
LOT 70 X125
INC (Y/N) Y   USE
ZONING RES

Style | R | RANCH
CONST ALUMINUM SIDED

Dir 176 TO RIVER RD. TO SUNSET (HOLIDAY HILLS) TO HOLIDAY TO EVERGREEN

Yr Blt 1974   Faces
ELEC 220 X   AMPS
Heat BASEBOA*   Fuel ELEC
IMP SEPTIC,CITY WATER
Mortgage 38,395   PITI 397
ASM% 8.5   Lender
Elem S. EDGEBROOK
Jr. Hi. MCHENRY
H.S. MCHENRY
Other MONTINI
Flood Hazard Ins. May Be Required.
R.O. RED CARPET-WESLEY
Ph 526-5488   # 817
S.P. SANDRA A. CRISPE
Ph 815-385-3110   # 1265

3.5%

#01283 $66,500

| Addr 9008 PINE AVE. | Map 0 | City MCHENRY | Zip 60050 | 86 02570 |
| Owner OF RECORD | | R RESIDENTIAL | RM 7 | BED 3 |

	F	L	C	W	Remarks LARGE HOME WITH SPACIOUS ROOMS
LR 15X15	U	Y			NEUTRALLY DECORATED. ADDITIONAL ROOM ON
DR					LOWER LEVEL COULD BE OFFICE OR 4TH BED-
KT 20X11	U	Y			ROOM LAUNDRY/UTILITY/MUD ROOM ALSO ON
FR 23X12	U	Y			LOWER LEVEL.
BR 16X11	U	Y			
11X10	U	Y			
11X09	U	Y			FOR APP'T CALL JOHNSBURG OFFICE
09X09	U	Y			815-385-8821
					LISTED IN MCHENRY FOR MLS ONLY
					LOCATED IN 60097
					WONDER LAKE P.O. MCHENRY COUNTY

BATH 1.5
AC
FPL WOOD,FAM RM
BSMT FULL,PART F*
GAR 1.5   ATTY   DETN
19 84   TAX
ASSMT 0
POSS ON CLOSING
LOT 150X60
INC (Y/N)   USE A
ZONING

Style | RR | RAISED RANCH
CONST

Dir RT 120 W TO THOMPSON RIGHT TO PINE AVE LEFT TO HOME ON RIGHT

Yr Blt   Faces
ELEC 220   AMPS
Heat F/A   Fuel GAS
IMP SEPTIC,CITY WATER
Mortgage   PITI
ASM%   Lender
Elem S. GREENWOOD
Jr. Hi. NORTHWOOD
H.S. WOODSTOCK
Other CATH
Flood Hazard Ins. May Be Required.
R.O. C21 CARE REAL ESTATE
Ph 815-344-1033   # 141
S.P. RONALD M. BYKOWSKI
Ph 815-385-4646   # 2064

3.5-20

EXPIRED LISTINGS

#01257 $42,900

Addr 601 COLUMBUS		Map 0	City MCHENRY	Zip 60050 86 00534
Owner OF RECORD			R RESIDENTIAL	RM 5 BED 3

	FL	C	W	Remarks ZONED B-1 THIS 3 BR HOME WITH	
LR 27 X 14	1			FIREPLACE OFFERS A 2 CAR GARAGE	BATH 1
DR				CONVERTED INTO AN OFFICE AREA & SHOP.	AC
KT 12 X 11	1			(COULD BE CONVERTED BACK TO A GARAGE)	FPL WOOD
FR				ENCLOSED BREEZEWAY BETWEEN HOUSE AND	BSMT SLAB
BR 12.5 X 11	1			SHOP GIVE PRIVACY TO HOME & SEPARATE	GAR ATTN DETN
BR 13X9.2	1			ENTRANCE TO YOUR BUSINESS. LARGE ROOMS	19 85 TAX 856.70
BR 11X10.5	1			& LOT. A MUST TO SEE.	ASSMT 0
GAR 24X24	1				POSS 60DA CONTRACT
					LOT 108.9 X 120.75
					INC [Y/N] Y USE
					ZONING B-1

Style [R] RANCH
CONST CEMENT BLOCK

Dir RT.176 TO RIVER TO LILY LAKE TO COLUMBUS-TURN R TO FRITZSCHE RD. (CORNER HSE ON L SIDE

Yr Blt 1954   Faces
ELEC 220   AMPS
Heat F/A   Fuel GAS
IMP SEPTIC, WELL WATER
Mortgage   PITI
ASM%   Lender
Elem S. HILLTOP
Jr.Hi. MCHENRY
Hi.S. MCHENRY
Other MONTINI
Flood Hazard Ins. May Be Required.
R.O. RED CARPET-WESLEY
Ph 526-5488   # 817
S.P. SANDRA A. CRISPE
Ph 815-385-3110   # 1265

3.5%

Expired unsold 120 days

#01258   FHA VA $45,000

Addr 7512 ALGONQUIN		Map 0	City MCHENRY	Zip 60050 86 01508
Owner OTTO AND HILDEGARD MONTFORT			R RESIDENTIAL	RM 4 BED 2

	FL	C	W	Remarks ITS A WONDERFUL LIFE!	
LR 16 X 11	1	Y	Y	A GREAT PLACE TO GO JUST ONE HOUR FROM	BATH 1 1
DR				DOWNTOWN CHICAGO.LOCATED ON A BEAUTIFUL	AC
KT 11 X 9	1		Y	LANDSCAPED DOUBLE LOT BEAMS THIS	FPL
FR				SPRALING RANCH. PRIDE OF OWNERSHIP	BSMT PARTIAL
BR 10 X 9	1			BEAMS EVERYWHERE. OWNER IS A GARDENER	GAR 2.5 ATTN DETY
9 X 9	1			AND WILL PASS ON ITS TREASURES TO YOU.	19 TAX
				EXTRA LARGE GARAGE FOR BOAT AND CAR	ASSMT 50
				STORAGE. UTILITY AREA IN PARTIAL	POSS CLOSING
				BASEMENT.MAINTENANCE FREE INSIDE AND	LOT 92 X 110
				OUT FROM CERAMIC TILE KITCHEN TO KNOTTY	INC [Y/N] N USE A
				PINE BEDROOMS.A GREAT PLACE TO START	ZONING RES

Style [R] RANCH
CONST VINYL

Dir MCCULLOM LK RD R TO WONDERLAKE RD L ON ALGONQUIN TO HOUSE

Yr Blt 1952   Faces EAST
ELEC 220   AMPS
Heat F/A   Fuel GAS
IMP SEPTIC, WELL WATER
Mortgage   PITI
ASM%   Lender
Elem S. MCHENRY
Jr.Hi. MCHENRY
Hi.S. MCHENRY *
Other
Flood Hazard Ins. May Be Required.
R.O. STARCK & CO.
Ph 438-8883   # 733
S.P. ARLENE FIELDS
Ph 438-2173   # 1256

3.5

Expired unsold 90 days

MARKET ACTIVITY SUMMARY

LAKE COUNTY

THIS YEAR = JULY 1985 - DECEMBER 1985   LAST YEAR = JULY 1984 - DECEMBER 1984

RESIDENTIAL PROPERTIES ONLY

----- ZIP CODE 60002 -----

	2 BEDROOMS THIS YEAR	2 BEDROOMS LAST YEAR	3 BEDROOMS THIS YEAR	3 BEDROOMS LAST YEAR	4 BEDROOMS THIS YEAR	4 BEDROOMS LAST YEAR	OVER 4 BEDROOMS THIS YEAR	OVER 4 BEDROOMS LAST YEAR
ALL OFF MARKETS								
#UNITS	112	99	138	146	59	49	13	12
NOT SOLD OR UNDR CNTRCT								
#UNITS	48	58	63	104	33	37	9	11
AVERAGE LIST PRICE	59,677	61,926	89,549	92,178	116,875	117,932	105,111	120,327
UNDR CNTRCT								
#UNITS	14	0	15	0	4	0	1	0
AVERAGE LIST PRICE	41,521	0	85,660	0	137,575	0	395,000	0
AVERAGE MARKET TIME	111	0	88	0	76	0	66	0
SOLD								
#UNITS	50	41	60	42	22	12	3	1
DOLLAR VALUE	2,565,700	1,851,250	4,793,665	2,986,850	2,128,547	1,318,500	470,000	180,000
AVERAGE LIST PRICE	54,742	48,000	84,260	75,483	103,918	117,983	168,166	199,000
AVERAGE SALE PRICE	51,314	45,152	79,894	71,115	96,752	109,875	156,666	180,000
AVERAGE SALE TIME	110	95	104	95	117	122	134	141
AVERAGE DIFFERENCE (LIST TO SALE PRICE)	3,428	2,848	4,366	4,368	7,166	8,108	11,500	19,000
% OF LIST PRICE	93	94	94	94	93	93	93	90
FINANCING: % OF TOTAL MARKET								
CONVENTIONAL	40	56	60	52	50	83	66	0
CSH	22	9	11	7	4	8	33	100
VA	14	4	5	14	13	0	0	0
FHA	12	12	16	9	18	0	0	0
MISC.	10	17	5	16	9	8	0	0
ASSUMED	0	0	1	0	0	0	0	0
EXCHANGED	0	0	0	0	0	0	0	0
BLENDED	0	0	0	0	0	0	0	0
PUR MONY MTG	0	0	0	0	0	0	0	0
NOT REPORTED	2	0	0	0	4	0	0	0

----- ZIP CODE 60015 -----

	2 BEDROOMS THIS YEAR	2 BEDROOMS LAST YEAR	3 BEDROOMS THIS YEAR	3 BEDROOMS LAST YEAR	4 BEDROOMS THIS YEAR	4 BEDROOMS LAST YEAR	OVER 4 BEDROOMS THIS YEAR	OVER 4 BEDROOMS LAST YEAR
ALL OFF MARKETS								
#UNITS	2	2	5	2	1	0	0	1
NOT SOLD OR UNDR CNTRCT								
#UNITS	1	0	3	1	1	0	0	1
AVERAGE LIST PRICE	114,900	0	122,166	122,900	159,500	0	0	219,900
UNDR CNTRCT								
#UNITS	1	0	0	0	0	0	0	0
AVERAGE LIST PRICE	84,000	0	0	0	0	0	0	0
AVERAGE MARKET TIME	1	0	0	0	0	0	0	0
SOLD								
#UNITS	0	2	2	1	0	0	0	0
DOLLAR VALUE	0	166,000	245,000	128,500	0	0	0	0
AVERAGE LIST PRICE	0	89,500	124,400	136,500	0	0	0	0
AVERAGE SALE PRICE	0	83,000	122,500	128,500	0	0	0	0
AVERAGE SALE TIME	0	309	12	16	0	0	0	0
AVERAGE DIFFERENCE (LIST TO SALE PRICE)	0	6,500	1,900	8,000	0	0	0	0
% OF LIST PRICE	0	92	98	94	0	0	0	0
FINANCING: % OF TOTAL MARKET								
CONVENTIONAL	0	50	100	0	0	0	0	0
CSH	0	50	0	100	0	0	0	0
VA	0	0	0	0	0	0	0	0
FHA	0	0	0	0	0	0	0	0
MISC.	0	0	0	0	0	0	0	0
ASSUMED	0	0	0	0	0	0	0	0
EXCHANGED	0	0	0	0	0	0	0	0
BLENDED	0	0	0	0	0	0	0	0
PUR MONY MTG	0	0	0	0	0	0	0	0
NOT REPORTED	0	0	0	0	0	0	0	0

Reprinted with permission of the Lake County Board of REALTORS®, Lake Villa, IL.

LONDAY

Real Estate Company

SUGGESTED REPAIRS AND IMPROVEMENTS
14622 Division

Paint the living room, dining room and hall an off-white
shade.

Clean the carpets in the living room, dining room, hall
and master bedroom.

Strip the wallpaper in the northeast bedroom and paint the
entire room in a neutral color.

Replace the six-foot section of sunken sidewalk west of the
driveway.

Remove two pieces of furniture from the family room.   The
amount of furniture in the family room makes it
appear smaller than it is.

Suite 402, Hillcrest Landing, Omaha, NE 68127
(402) 733-5443

LONDAY

Real Estate Company

SUGGESTED FINANCING TO IMPROVE MARKETABILITY

1) Allow your present FHA mortgage to be assumed on the condition that the purchaser provide you with a release of liability. Cost to you: $35.

2) Carryback $10,000 at 12 percent amortized over 30 years with a five-year balloon payment, using a trust deed as security for the loan. Your net from the second trust deed would be as follows:

Principal and Interest for 60 months
    at $102.86: $ 6,171.60

Principal Balance to be paid after
    the 60th payment: 9,766.39

Total Principal and Interest received
over 60 months: $15,937.99

Suite 402, Hillcrest Landing, Omaha, NE 68127
(402) 733-5443

LONDAY
Real Estate Company

SELLER'S ESTIMATE SHEET
(Loan Assumption)

Name   Bob and Mary Seller

Property Address   14622 Division

Date   6/23   Price   59,900   Financing **Loan Assumption**
                                                        w/seller carryback

Existing Loan At: **First Trust**	32,540
Estimated Interest on Current Mortgage.................	244
Record Release of Current Mortgage....................	
Prepayment Fee on Current Mortgage....................	
Escrow Adjustment: Refund **XX** Shortage ____	- 540
Property Tax Adjustment: Refund **XX** Due ____	- 20
Brokerage Fee: 7 % of final sales price...............	4,193
Title Insurance/Examination of Abstract...............	120
Loan Discount Points: Currently ___% on $_____	
Termite Inspection (Seller pays on new VA loans only)..	
Revenue on Deed: 55¢ per $500 of sales price...........	66
Smoke Detectors Required by Law.......................	10
Special Assessments...................................	
Suggested Repairs.....................................	800
Release of Liability on FHA/VA assumptions............	35
Seller Carryback......................................	10,000
Second Mortgage Payoff Balance.......................	
Release of Second Mortgage...........................	
Total Estimated Costs.................................	47,458
Selling Price...	59,900
Estimated Seller's Costs and Prorations...............	47,448
Estimated Proceeds to the Seller.....................	12,452

Suite 402, Hillcrest Landing, Omaha, NE 68127
(402) 733-5443

LONDAY
Real Estate Company

SELLER'S ESTIMATE SHEET
(FHA or VA)

Name __Bob and Mary Seller__

Property Address __14622 Division__

Date __6/23__   Price __59,900__   Financing **New FHA or VA**
                                                            Financing

Existing Loan At: __First Trust__ 32,540

Estimated Interest on Current Mortgage................. 244

Record Release of Current Mortgage.................... 10

Prepayment Fee on Current Mortgage....................

Escrow Adjustment: Refund **XX** Shortage ____ .... − 540

Property Tax Adjustment: Refund **XX** Due ____ .... − 20

Brokerage Fee: 7% of final sales price................ 4,193

Title Insurance/Examination of Abstract.............. 120

Loan Discount Points: Currently __3__ % on $ __59,900__ 1,796

Termite Inspection (Seller pays on new VA loans only).. 35

Revenue on Deed: 55¢ per $500 of sales price.......... 66

Smoke Detectors Required by Law...................... 10

Special Assessments..................................

Suggested Repairs.................................... 800

Release of Liability on FHA/VA assumptions............

Seller Carryback....................................

Second Mortgage Payoff Balance.......................

Release of Second Mortgage...........................

Total Estimated Costs................................ 39,255

Selling Price.. 59,900

Estimated Seller's Costs and Prorations.............. 39,255

Estimated Proceeds to the Seller..................... 20,645

Suite 402, Hillcrest Landing, Omaha, NE 68127
(402) 733-5443

REAL ESTATE CAREER DEVELOPMENT INSTITUTE

SUITE 402, HILLCREST LANDING ATRIUM ● 7500 MAIN, OMAHA, NE 68127 ● 402-339-2380

HOW DISCOUNT POINTS WORK

VA-guaranteed loans have a maximum interest rate set by the Veterans Administration. This rate is periodically changed to reflect market conditions. Rates are normally adjusted so that they are somewhat below prevailing conventional mortgage rates.

To make up the difference between the maximum VA rate and the prevailing conventional rates, the loan companies charge what are called discount points. One point is equal to one percent of the new loan balance. These points are charged to and paid for by the seller on VA loans.

FHA loans do not have a maximum rate; however, discount points still are paid in most cases. They are negotiable, meaning they can be paid by the seller or buyer. Frequently, through negotiation, the seller is asked to pay the points on FHA loans simply because the buyers do not have the money. Buyers are not allowed to add the cost of discount points to their new loan.

No seller wants to pay discount points. However, studies have shown that houses sold with FHA or VA financing in which the sellers pay points consistently sell for higher prices than properties sold using other types of financing. Although the seller is charged with this expense on the settlement sheet, in reality the buyer is paying for most, if not all, of the cost of the points in the form of a higher selling price.

This is substantiated by a study conducted by the Center for Applied Urban Research, a branch of the University of Nebraska at Omaha. The study found that 96 percent of the cost of FHA discount points are returned to the seller in the form of higher selling prices, while 80 percent of the cost of VA points are returned to sellers through higher prices.

Discount point studies have also been conducted in Columbus, Ohio and Lubbock, Texas. While the three studies came up with slightly different percentages, they all came to the same conclusion: The majority of discount points are paid by buyers through higher selling prices.

JAMES K. LONDAY, DIRECTOR

PRE AND POST LICENSING INSTRUCTION/SEMINARS/SPEAKING ENGAGEMENTS

SAMPLE "OPEN HOUSE" BROCHURE

OPEN
SUNDAY
1:00 - 3:00

14622 Division

Great loan assumption with possible seller carryback on the immaculate six-year-old split entry. Large country kitchen fully equipped with self-cleaning range/oven, dishwasher, and disposal. Full wall brick fireplace in the lower-level family room. Large deck. Chain link–fenced rear yard. Walking distance to public and parochial grade and high schools. Location! Condition! Financing! It's got it all! For additional information or to arrange a private showing, call Jim Londay at 555-2380 or 555-5443.

Sample "Salesperson" Brochure

NEW LISTING
14622 Division

Great loan assumption with possible seller carryback on the immaculate six-year-old split entry. Full-wall brick fireplace in the lower-level family room. Location! Condition! Financing! It's got it all! Call Jim Londay at 555-2380 or 555-5443 for additional information.

# BR **three**			# BA **1 ½**				$ **59,900**	
RESIDENTIAL								
Ad **14622 Division**						L #		
Style **SPRT**		Poss **Nego**	Oc **O**	Age **6**	Area **162**		Bk **S/77**	
C	D	L	Room Size	2 Car Gar **BI**	SID **207**		LB **OBR**	
x	x	1	LR **13.6 x 12**	B% **100**	WO **--**	CC **.028**		
v	x	1	DR **11.9 x 8.6**	Ext **w**	FP **yes**	1 Mtg **1st Land Trust**		
v	x	1	Kit **8.6 x 11.9**	RF **c**	HT **GFA**	Mtg. Bal **32,540**		
x	x	B	FR **22.6 x 11.2**	Fen **c1**	CA **yes**	Type **FHA**	Int **9**	
			RR	Pav **yes**	P/l **yes**	$ **362.00**	T **x**	l **x**
x	x	1	BR **11.3x13.6**	Swr **yes**	R/O **yes**	Tax 19	$ **940.22**	
x	x	1	BR **11.10x10.6**	Wtr **yes**	Dsh **yes**	LC	WRAP	**xx**
x	x	1	BR **10.6x9.6**	Gas **yes**	Disp **yes**	SA	**xx** CASH	**xx**
			BR	BA **1 ½**		LA/GVT	**xx** CNV	**xx**
Grd **Pawnee**				J Hi **Bryan**	LA/OTH	CNV 10	**xx**
Par **St Bernadette**			Hi **Bryan**	VA	**xx** CNV 5	**xx**
Legal **Lot 427, Glenmorrie**				FHA	**xx** 2 FL **--**	
			Lot Sz. **70x115**			EML **1028**	FIN. B **252**	
Remarks **Exceptionally neat and clean**							FSF **1280**	

Seller will carry back $10,000 @ 12% over 30 yrs w/a balloon after 5 years. Release of Liability required

B #**7349**	P 555-2380	A **Jim Londay**	R 555-5443

This information, although believed to be accurate, is not guaranteed.

LONDAY
Real Estate Company

"THANKS FOR SHOWING MY LISTING"

(place a photocopy of a
picture of the property here)

Thanks for showing the above property located at: _____

The owner and I would appreciate your frank feedback. Please
provide us with the following to the extent of your knowledge.

What did your prospect think the house was worth? _____

What do you feel the market value is? _____

If known, please state why your prospect did not buy this house.

_____

_____

_____

Do you have any suggestions to improve the marketability of
the property?

_____

_____

_____

The source of this information will be kept strictly confidential.
Please return your comments in the enclosed, stamped envelope.
Your assistance in helping us amrket this property correctly is
appreciated.

Sincerely,

Suite 402, Hillcrest Landing, Omaha, NE 68127
(402) 733-5443

LONDAY
Real Estate Company

PROPOSED MARKETING SCHEDULE

14622 Division

6/25   Listing will be distributed to all Londay Real Estate Co. salespersons.

6/27   Listing will appear in the multiple listing service computer.

7/1   House will be toured by Londay Co. salespersons.

7/8   Photo ad will appear in "Metro Homes" magazine.

7/13   200 open-house ads will be mailed to all residents of Glenmorrie.

7/15   400 promotional brochures will be mailed to salespersons active in the Sarpy area.

7/19   Open house for the public will be help from 1:00 to 3:00. An open house classified ad will be run on that date.

7/22   Photo ad again will appear in "Metro Homes" magazine.

Suite 402, Hillcrest Landing, Omaha, NE 68127
(402) 733-5443

COMPLETED LISTING AGREEMENT

MULTIPLE LISTING SERVICE
LAKE COUNTY BOARD OF REALTORS®
EXCLUSIVE RIGHT TO SELL AGREEMENT

1 IN CONSIDERATION OF SERVICES to be performed by __Londay Real Estate Company, Suite 402 Hillcrest__
2 ___Landing___ _(Realtor®)   _(Address)
3 hereinafter called Realtor®, the Seller or their legal agent hereby authorizes and irrevocably gives the Realtor® the EXCLUSIVE RIGHT TO SELL the herein
4 described property.

5 LISTING ADDRESS and/or LEGAL DESCRIPTION __14622 Division__
6 _____ Omaha, NE _____
7 _____
8 _____

9 PRICE AND TERMS $ __59,900 - Cash, Conventional, FHA, VA, Loan Assumption__
10 or other price and/or terms as Seller may agree to accept.

11 POSSESSION (strike inapplicable): ~~at closing~~ ~~XXXXXXXXXXXX~~ (other) __negotiable__
12 INCLUDED IN SALE are the following items, if any, now on the premises: screens; storm windows and doors, shades and blinds; drapery rods; curtain rods;
13 radiator covers; attached TV antennas; attached mirrors; shelving, shutters, cabinets and bookcases, awnings; water softener; planted vegetation; garage door
14 openers and transmitters; attached fireplace screens; wall to wall carpet. _____
15 _____
16 _____

17 SELLER GRANTS REALTOR® SOLE AUTHORITY to advertise, display signs consistent with applicable ordinances, provide information regarding property to
18 MLS, and sell property for a period of _____ six _____ months. Seller hereby authorizes Realtor® to install lock box on
19 property. This listing expires at midnight on __November 30, 1986__ _____ unless extended by separate written
20 agreement between Seller and Realtor®.

21 **REALTOR® AGREES:** to inspect property. To compile and have available all sales information and to assist in financing arrangements. To take prospective pur-
22 chasers through the property at convenient times, To make a continued and earnest effort to sell the property. To advertise the property as he deems advisable in
23 order to obtain prospective purchasers. Within 72 hours of receipt to send information concerning this property to the LAKE COUNTY BOARD OF REALTORS®

24 MULTIPLE LISTING SERVICE for dissemination to participants therein; and to invite such participants to inspect the property on __May 15, 1986__(date).
25 Realtors® sole duty is to effect a sale of the property and is not charged with the custody, management, maintenance, upkeep or repair.

26 **SELLER AGREES:** To cooperate fully, provide access to property for purpose of showing, refer all inquiries and conduct all negotiations through Realtor®, to
27 furnish a commitment for title insurance in the amount of the sale price at least five (5) days prior to closing, as evidence of merchantible title, to pay a real estate

28 brokerage commission to Realtor® of __seven percent__ _____ of the sale price,
29 (1) if Realtor® provides a purchaser ready, willing and able to purchase in accordance with this agreement, or (2) if the property is sold, exchanged, gifted or
30 optioned by Realtor, Seller, or by or through any other person during the period of this agreement, or (3) if after termination of this agreement it is sold within six
31 months directly or indirectly to a purchaser to whom it was offered during the term hereof unless the property is listed exclusively with another broker, or (4) if in
32 the event of an installment sale upon execution of the Articles of Agreement for Warranty Deed. The commission shall be paid at closing or if there is no closing,
33 then Seller agrees to pay such commission as may be due to Realtor® under this agreement upon written demand to Seller by Realtor®. Seller shall indemnify and
34 save and hold Realtor and Realtor's agents harmless from all claims, litigations, judgements and costs arising from any misrepresentations made by the Seller,
35 incorrect information supplied by Seller or problems with the property which are known to the Seller and Seller fails to disclose. Seller agrees that at the closing of
36 property which are known to the Seller and Seller fails to disclose. Seller agrees that at the closing of the sale of this property, or as many be otherwise agreed, the
37 Realtor® may pay out of the escrow funds if any, the commission as set forth above and any additional expenses as agreed to by the Seller.

38 It is understood by Seller that the Realtor® is a member of the LAKE COUNTY BOARD OF REALTORS® and is a participant in the MULTIPLE LISTING SERVICE
39 thereof. It is Sellers desire that this listing be processed and circulated to all participants in said Service, and the Realtor® is authorized and instructed to submit
40 this agreement, and any subsequent authorized additions or changes, to said Service in a timely manner.

41 **SELLER AGREES:** To furnish a certified survey, as required in a contract for sale, by a licensed land surveyor showing the location of all improvements to be with-
42 in the lot lines, and that there are no encroachments of other improvements from adjoining properties. Seller shall execute and deliver or cause to be executed
43 and delivered to purchaser a proper instrument of conveyance upon payment of agreed purchase price, said conveyance to be subject only to title exceptions as
44 set forth in the contract to purchase.

45 If sold under FHA or VA approval, Seller agrees to pay lenders discount not to exceed __nego__ % of the loan amount.

46 **SELLER WARRANTS:** His authority to execute this agreement on behalf of said property as herein provided, that there are no known unpaid special assessments
47 and none confirmed relative to the property except those amounting to approximately $ __none__
48 for _____
49 which Seller agrees to pay. No notice has been received from any government authority of any dwelling code violation affecting the property which has not been
50 cured. Seller agrees to comply with all zoning and occupancy regulations as may be required by the appropriate governmental authority. Seller shall provide
51 sufficient maintenance of the property, including landscaping, so that, upon tender of possession the property shall be in the same condition as at the date of
52 signing of a purchase contract by Buyer, less ordinary wear and tear, broom clean and free of debris.

53 **GENERAL PROVISIONS: In the event of default by purchaser, earnest money (if any) shall be** forfeited and first applied to payment of broker's commission and
54 **any expenses authorized by Seller** incurred by broker, and balance paid to Seller. At Sellers election such forfeiture may be in full settlement of all Seller's
55 damages. If Seller defaults, earnest money, at option of Purchaser, shall be refunded to Purchaser, but such refunding shall not release Seller from the obligation
56 of this contract.

57 It is understood that it is illegal for either the Seller or Realtor® to refuse to display to, or sell to, any person because of their race, color, religion, national origin,
58 sex or physical disability.

59 It is mutually understood and agreed that, by law, Realtor® is only permitted to prepare a contract of sale. Seller agrees to furnish or have an attorney furnish all
60 legal documents necessary to close the transaction

61 It is mutually understood and agreed that (a) This agreement shall be binding upon and inure to the benefit of the heirs, executors, administrators, successors,
62 and assigns of the parties hereto. (b) No amendments or alterations in the terms of this agreement with respect to the amount of commission or with respect to the
63 time of payment of commission shall be valid or binding unless made in writing and signed by all the parties hereto. (c) This agreement shall take precedence
64 over any other listing (whether exclusive or not) which is prior in time and which has expired in accordance with its terms and conditions. (d) If more than one
65 purchaser or seller are involved, or if the Realtor® is an entity other than a natural person, the pronouns and grammatical structure shall be understood to
66 conform.

Realtor® __Londay Real Estate Company__

__Suite 402 Hillcrest Landing__ _(Seller) __Robert Seller__ _____ (Seal)
        _(Address)

                              _(Seller) __Mary Seller__ _____ (Seal)
By _____ (Seal) Seller's home address __14622 Division__
Date __Jim Londay__ __May 1, 1986__   __Omaha, NE__

Distribution (1st copy-Realtor®) — (2nd copy-MLS Office) — (3rd copy-Seller)   Form # 101-12-82-25M

CHAPTER 7

GETTING THE LISTING

This chapter teaches the attitudes, techniques, and dialogue needed to give a professional listing presentation.

THE CONTINUOUS-CLOSE TECHNIQUE

Although trial and final closes are included, the presentation from start to finish should be considered one continuous close. All inclusions and dialogue should move you closer to a signed listing agreement—your main goal. Any part of your presentation that does not move your prospects toward this goal should be eliminated. Preparation and easy-to-understand dialogue put you in control throughout the presentation. In a well-done presentation, control of the direction and flow will be accomplished without using high pressure.

The salesperson naturally does most of the talking during a listing presentation. Verbally, the salesperson is twice as active as the prospect. Nonverbally, the salesperson should "listen" more than he or she talks. To gain the trust of the sellers and do the best job possible for them, a salesperson needs to learn at least as much from the prospects as they learn from the salesperson. Understanding your prospects' feelings and emotions is essential. Determine the way they view their situation. Finding out how they see things allows you to answer their questions, calm their fears, and eliminate their concerns.

Monitor your prospects' reactions to what you are saying. Try to pick up on any concerns they have as they arise. These concerns, real or baseless, are dealt with most effectively at the time they come up. If not met and solved immediately, they will divert your prospect's thoughts, causing him or her to tune you out. Be flexible; alter your presentation in midstream to handle problems that will tend to divert the prospect's attention. If you do not, these unresolved concerns will reappear as roadblocks when you attempt to get the listing agreement signed.

This presentation anticipates and diffuses the most common objections encountered when trying to list a house. You should not regularly experience objections at the final close. If you do, you are not sensing and resolving your prospects' concerns along the way.

The pace of your presentation is important. People absorb information at widely differing rates. Do not make the prospect adjust to your pace. Present the material at a pace with which your prospect is comfortable. This creates the best climate in which to explain the basis and results of your market analysis, giving you the best chance possible to obtain the customer's business.

In many cases, the customer will not be interested in a detailed analysis of the data you have assembled. Other prospects will want to study each phase of the presentation in detail. Train yourself to be consciously aware of your prospects' attention level. Adjust the tempo to keep the prospects' involvement at a peak.

Make every portion of the presentation a trial close by arriving at a full understanding with the prospect before you move on. This is true whether you are discussing the price at which property is listed, when the open house is to be held, how often the property is to be advertised, and so on through every phase of the presentation. Even though you will not present the actual listing agreement until the end of your presentation, you are in effect asking for the signature every time you confirm a point during the presentation. **You must reach full agreement on every point of the presentation before moving on if you are to avoid objections when going for the signature.**

A salesperson needs to be operating at 100 percent efficiency to give the best presentation possible. Train yourself to focus your concentration on the task at hand whenever working with prospects. Make a dedicated effort to concentrate fully. A calm, relaxed, and confident appearance is essential because the prospect's attitude will largely reflect your attitude. If you are obviously nervous, the prospect will be uneasy. On the other hand, if you appear at ease and comfortable with the material presented, the prospect will be relaxed, too.

Creating the impression of being skilled and confident in what you are doing is the best way to sell yourself. Learning to do this is not easy. The ability to project the impression that you are knowledgeable and in control is achieved through practice, experience, preparation, and a thorough knowledge of the real estate business as it applies to the situation.

New salespersons should give as many listing presentations to actual prospects as possible, even if the listing prospects are not highly motivated. Working with real prospects has no substitute. Preparing and presenting a market analysis to a real prospect, even a poorly motivated one, improves your presentation skills.

You can benefit each time you do a listing presentation by honestly evaluating how every phase of the presentation was received. Do this immediately after the appointment and again over the next few days. If you pay attention to your prospects' reactions, you will know when you hit a clinker. You will not be the first person to experience a sticking point in a listing presentation. After the presentation, analyze what led up to it, what caused it, and decide what new approach you will use to avoid it in the future. You may need help in remedying the problem for future presentations. Talk to your manager or to fellow salespersons whose opinions you respect. A colleague may provide the very dialogue or approach you will find effective, or you may need to get more than one opinion. Do not hesitate to approach top-producing listers. They have the ability to help you and are usually the first to share their knowledge. Incorporate what you learn in your future presentations.

You will learn, grow, and improve only by trying new approaches, ideas, and phrases. Vary your presentation. Critique each presentation in a positive way and incorporate needed changes. You will continually improve your professional skills and the results you receive. The beauty of the continuous-close technique is that you will get the listing in the vast majority of cases you apply it after you learn to tailor it to individual prospects.

Extensive presentation is included in this section to teach you concepts, ideas, and attitudes. Although a salesperson may want to learn and remember key phrases, memorizing the presentation in this chapter is not recommended. It is included to teach you the concepts and techniques you need to educate your prospects, gain their trust, and obtain their business. For best results, put the principles in this chapter into your own words.

The listing packet itself should be viewed as a roadmap to follow toward your destination of a signed listing agreement. It is the focal point of your verbal presentation. A salesperson should know the material in it well enough to present it fluently without reciting memorized dialogue. A memorized speech carries little credibility.

INTRODUCING THE PRESENTATION

When you arrive for the actual presentation, take time to set the stage. Get acquainted with any of the sellers you have not met previously and take a few minutes to establish a comfortable relationship with them. When the introductions are complete, suggest that sitting at the kitchen or dining room table would be best. Family business usually is discussed and conducted there and your prospects will be most comfortable in this setting. Sitting at a table allows you to spread out materials, illustrate facts and figures on scratch paper, and ease the act of obtaining the prospects' signatures on the listing agreement.

The only items you should have with you are the folder containing your presentation, a current listing book, and your appointment book. Many people are intimidated by a briefcase. Your goal is to put them at ease, so leave your briefcase at home or in your car.

Set the stage with an introduction similar to the following before opening the folder, passing out materials, and discussing specifics about the prospects' house:

> "Mr. and Mrs. Seller, my job is to get as much money as possible for you as quickly as I can from the sale of your property. I view myself as the employee, working for you, the employer. I am here to give you all the information you need to make an informed decision on how your property is to be marketed. After you have made that decision my goal will be to work with you in every way I can to produce as quick a sale as possible at the top of the fair range of value for your house. Before talking about how we can best accomplish this goal, I would like to share some basic

marketing principles that will help you decide how you want your property marketed.

"Although as sellers you do not determine what the market value of your property is—the marketplace itself does that—you will decide, when you place your house on the market, how fast it will sell by what you price it at, the condition you have it in, and the financing terms you offer to prospective purchasers. These three factors are the overriding determinants of how quickly a property sells.

"Among professional appraisers, it is generally acknowledged that every parcel of real estate has a price range of approximately ten percent in which a sale would be fair for both the seller and the buyer. Correctly determining this fair range is very important when pricing the property. Best results for the seller are obtained by placing the property on the market at the top of its fair range of value. This provides the best chance for a quick sale at top dollar.

"Pricing a property above the top of its fair range hurts the seller because it greatly reduces the number of showings. Naturally the fewer buyers who view the house, the longer it will take to sell. The closer a property is priced to its fair market value, the more quickly it will generally sell; this is a basic marketing fact.

"A seller will not receive more by overpricing the property. Final market value is determined by active buyers in the marketplace, not by real estate salespersons, sellers, or asking price. Overpricing a property relative to its value does only two things. One, it lengthens the time the house sits on the market before a buyer is found. If overpriced enough, properties don't sell at all. Two, it helps sell all the other properties for sale in the area that are priced right.

"The best time to sell any parcel of property is in the first month to six weeks it is on the market. After two months have gone by, the house becomes what professionals in the business refer to as 'stale.' It develops a stigma, even among salespersons who have not been in the house. In most cases a significant price reduction is necessary to sell a property after it has this stigma. Houses in this category often sell for less than they could have if they had been priced correctly when first placed on the market."

Continue the presentation in this manner:

"The asking price of a property is the most important of the factors over which a seller has control. You see, Mr. and Mrs. Seller, there are only four reasons a property does not sell. They are: location, condition, financing terms offered, and price. Of course, location is a factor we cannot control, leaving condition, terms, and price the only items we control when selling a house.

"The condition of a property influences whether it sells for top dollar or not. Generally speaking, getting the highest possible net from the sale of a house is obtained by having the property in top condition. The market value of a house is influenced by its present condition, not the condition it would be in if needed repairs and redecoration were completed. We will discuss how this relates to your house later.

"The type of financing offered is also an important factor. Buyers buy payments, not price. For a property to sell at the top of its fair range, it must have terms that are competitive with other properties currently on the market.

"This leaves price, the most important factor we control. Unfortunately there is no way anyone can predict the exact market value of your house. This is found only by placing the property on the market, promoting it aggressively, and allowing enough time to let the marketplace tell us how much the house is worth. We place it on the market at the top of the fair range because that ensures that we are not underpricing your house, while allowing us to let the marketplace provide us enough feedback to decide if we are priced correctly or not.

"To estimate the fair range of value for your house, we look at recent sales of properties similar to yours. I limited the use of sold properties to those in the same geographical area as your house. I also restricted them to properties sold in the last six to nine months. I realize none of these houses are exactly like yours and that your property has some advantages some of these others do not. I made adjustments as best I could for the relative advantages and disadvantages of each property as it compares to yours. The sold properties I chose are the most appropriate I could locate. They provide the most valid basis available to estimate your property's probable market value.

"Having covered these basic marketing principles, I would like to start reviewing specific market data and how they relate to your situation."

As noted earlier, avoid using the terms "comp" or "comparable." These terms are vague and sometimes have a negative connotation to people not in the real estate business.

PRESENTING THE MARKET ANALYSIS

At this point, open the presentation folder and remove all the contents. Place the contents on top of the empty folder. Set aside the cover sheet, in view of the prospects. It needs no comment. Distribute copies of the computer printout summary to everyone at the table. Say something similar to:

> "This first sheet is a computer printout of market activity in your subdivision. It summarizes properties sold in the last year, houses currently on the market, the number of pending sales at this time, and all property listings that expired unsold in the last year. I included this to give you a feel for how rapidly and how often property is selling in your neighborhood."

Briefly discuss the total number in each category and how they relate. This indirectly informs your prospects that all properties do not sell and that they will experience competition from other properties when marketing theirs. Do not discuss individual properties from this list. It serves only as an overview.

After you have covered the computer printout summary, pass out copies of the subject property data sheet and a complete set of comps. Proceed as follows:

> "These are the properties I selected on which to base my analysis. As you can see, they are all the same basic floor plan and approximately the same square footage as your house. Each is located in your subdivision and was sold within the last nine months.
>
> "Also included is a page detailing the information I gathered on your house. Our goal is to objectively compare your house to these houses that have sold to help us decide what the best price is to market your house."

Discuss each property and how it relates to your prospects' house to the extent your prospects are interested. If they wish, conduct an in-depth discussion of each final sold and how it relates to theirs. In most cases the prospects want only a brief review of the comparables as a whole. Let them spend all the time they want reviewing the comps. Do not tell the sellers at this time what you feel the market value of their property is.

After the solds have been covered to the prospects' satisfaction, distribute the "current pendings," preceding them with a statement similar to:

> "This is a summary of properties recently for sale for which a buyer has been found, but whose sales have not been closed yet. These properties are similar to yours in style, size, and location."

Discuss these properties in the same way you covered the final solds. Take the time to call the listing or selling salespersons involved in the sales to get details if they are not available through your multiple-listing service.

Next, pass out copies of the current "on markets" to the prospects:

> "The following are copies of listings for houses currently on the market in the same area as your house. I want to strongly stress that what these properties are priced at has no direct bearing on their market value. It is a fact that there is virtually no discernible relationship between asking price and market value. Asking price merely reflects the extent of the knowledge the sellers have of the real estate market and their level of motivation.
>
> "The reason we are looking at these properties is to make sure we are not pricing your property too high in relationship to the competition. (Pause) That is correct: As sellers, you have to look at all other properties for sale at this time in this area as your competition.
>
> "Best results for a seller are obtained by pricing the property below the asking prices of similar houses in the area, as long as they do not price the property below the top of its fair range. As long as it is not underpriced, marketing a property at a price below the competition will ensure increased showing traffic and, in most cases, a quicker sale. This approach will not result in a lower net to the seller. On the contrary, in many cases a seller will net more by pricing a property this way when it is first placed on the market.
>
> "Occasionally, sellers want to price their property at an unrealistically high price, hoping to 'get lucky' and find someone willing to pay more than the house could reasonably be worth. The marketplace just does not work that way. In this age of consumerism, potential house buyers are the most thorough comparative shoppers in the marketplace.

"In no instance is it advisable to price a house above the asking prices of similar properties. Doing so virtually eliminates showing traffic and reduces the possibilities of a sale to almost nothing.

"Let's review these properties, keeping in mind that the prices on them do not reflect their market value. To put them in the proper perspective, we want to look at them through a potential buyer's eyes. Remember that buyers have access to this same information and will use it when deciding what properties they are going to look at."

Discuss the properties in general, spending additional time on individual houses you feel are particularly relevant. Express your opinion on whether these properties are priced competitively or not, always injecting into the conversation the thought that some of the properties remain unsold even though they seem to be priced correctly.

When finished with the on-markets, distribute the expireds:

"Mr. and Mrs. Seller, this last group of properties was on the market during the past year and expired unsold during the entire period they were listed. Multiple-listing service statistics tell us that one out of every four houses placed on the market with a real estate salesperson in the last year expired unsold (use the current figure for your locality).

"Let's review these properties to look for traits that prevented them from selling. Although we can't determine the exact reason each one did not sell, we can see that generally speaking there were higher asking prices on the properties that did not sell than on those that did sell."

Let the prospects briefly review the expireds. Your point will be reinforced if they recognize any of the properties in this group. Do not dwell on this group. Stay with it only long enough to make the point that not all properties placed on the market sell.

Distribute copies of the market activity summary. Explain this paper and its contents as follows:

"Mr. and Mrs. Seller, this is a summary of house sales for the metropolitan area (town, county, so on). It contains the statistics for all real estate sales in this area during the last six months. It also gives totals for all properties currently on the market. The first area I would like you to look at is the summary of sold properties."

The method of explanation you use will differ depending on what statistics are released by your multiple-listing service and how they are released. Be sure to include and explain these statistics if they are available:

1. the number of final sales (City or areawide figures are almost always available. Many times, statistics are broken down by multiple-listing area, price ranges, types of houses, etc.);
2. the average percentage or amount of negotiation between listing price and final sales price;
3. the average time on the market before a buyer is found; and
4. the percentage of properties that expire unsold and go off the market. (Note: Some multiple-listing service computers can now provide this information for specific areas of a city.)

Decide what statistics to include and how much explanation you want to give. When finished with discussing the sold properties, move on to the current on-the-markets:

> "This section summarizes all houses currently on the market. These are the properties that potential buyers will compare to your house. They are broken down this way: . . ."

Provide a brief explanation of the statistics you consider important. Try to include the number of properties on the market, both citywide and for the area your seller's house is in (if available). Include statistics on average asking prices and average time on the market for unsold houses.

Proceed to the summary of current market activity. Explain the rate of sales (pendings per week, month, or whatever period is available) and how it compares to the number of houses for sale. Break it down to a statistic the average seller can understand:

> "If we divide the number of houses on the market by the average number of sales per week, we can see that the chances of any particular property selling during any one-week period are one in 16."

Explain discernible trends in the rate of sales, changes of average time on the market, or any other trends that will make your prospects more aware of current market conditions and what they can expect when they place their property on the market.

Suggested Improvements

If you feel your sellers should make improvements to their property, start with an explanation:

> "As we discussed briefly, one of the factors in selling a property at the top of its market value is to put and keep it in excellent condition. Having a property in top condition when marketing it is important because prospective buyers discount what they will pay for a property that needs work. This hurts the seller because, in most cases, properties that need work sell for far less than their true market value. The penalty the marketplace puts on houses in this category is out of proportion to the cost of the needed work. A house that is basically in good shape but needs $1,000 worth of paint and carpet will often sell for $4,000 less than it should, penalizing the seller $3,000 because of a failure to do $1,000 worth of cosmetic work.
>
> "Experience also tells us that sellers who wait to do needed work until weeks after their house goes on the market hurt themselves by creating a time dilemma. They suppress market activity by waiting to do needed work. Properties in anything less than top condition discourage showing activity and produce a negative reaction among buyers. Lack of market activity disheartens sellers. They lose precious marketing time and are many times forced to take the first offer that comes along. Because of this they often net less than they could have if they had done the needed work when the house was first placed on the market.
>
> "Basically, your house is in very good condition and I have only a few suggestions for improvements."

Distribute copies of the suggested repair summary and explain:

> "I have outlined some specific recommendations. I feel that these improvements will help you sell the house at the best price possible at the soonest possible date."

Discuss in detail exactly what you would like done. If any of the work is major, have a list of repairmen or contractors the owners can contact to obtain bids. Inform them that you do not receive a referral fee from these people and that you are recommending them only because they have proven track records.

Ask for a commitment. Be direct and ask for it in such a way that it also will serve as a trial close:

> "Mr. and Mrs. Seller, no matter who sells your property, it is in your best interests to get this work done. Would it be feasible for you to have it completed before an open house is held? Perhaps in the next two or three weeks?"

Do not force the issue. If they are adamant about not doing the work, drop it. Do not let the suggested repairs become such an issue that you lose the listing. At least you have laid the groundwork for changes in price or condition at a later date if the property does not sell.

Financing Options

If you are trying to land a listing in times of high interest rates, you may want to suggest alternate financing options to your seller:

> "As you know, mortgage interest rates are extremely high now. Sellers willing to offer alternative financing options to help reduce the buyer's payment are experiencing quicker sales than sellers who do not. In your situation I would recommend you consider offering the following options."

Start by explaining the options you would like them to offer. When they understand them generally, produce a sheet detailing how they would affect their personal situation. Provide a detailed breakdown including a projection of initial costs, initial net, ongoing net, and total net the seller can expect. Be frank in discussing the advantages and disadvantages. Explain to your prospects that if they have enough time, they could choose to test the waters, not offering this option initially, but with the thought of possibly adding it later if market activity is not acceptable. Gauge your sellers' reaction when deciding how far to carry this discussion. If you discern even vague discomfort, move on, knowing you have planted the seed of the idea.

THE SELLER'S ESTIMATE SHEET

You are now ready to introduce the seller's net sheet. Before presenting it, set the stage:

> "I used the information we discussed in arriving at my opinion of your property's market value. Based on your property's location, its condition after the repairs are made, and offering the terms we are discussing, I feel the top market value of your property is $79,900."

Wait for their reaction. If announcing your figure produces merely mild disappointment, you are doing fine. If you sense real pain or disagreement, address the problem. When you get an obvious negative reaction, the price issue must be resolved before proceeding.

Frequently your sellers will feel your figure is too low, even though you have provided market data supporting your suggested price. Put the ball in their court:

> "Mr. Seller, you may be correct in thinking your property is worth more than $79,900. Perhaps there are other sales or factors involved of which I am not aware. What is your basis for thinking your house is worth $88,000?"

Tread softly. This is a delicate situation. Proceed in a relaxed way, again reviewing the comps and market data you brought. In the rare instance in which your seller has additional information, include it in the discussion. As best you can, arrive at an agreement on the price at which the house should be marketed. Get the price as close as you can to your suggested price without losing the listing. Work hard at getting the property priced as correctly as possible, as price is the most important factor in marketing success. Do not proceed until you have reached agreement on the figure at which the property should be priced.

Upon reaching agreement on a market value, distribute the seller's estimate sheet. Complete it in advance based upon your suggested marketing price. Discuss it with the prospects, item by item. Many homeowners will need no explanation of most of the costs. Touch lightly on any inclusions your prospects already understand. Explain the others to the necessary extent. The following sections include suggested statements to use on each item on the estimate sheet.

Existing loan

"Mr. and Mrs. Seller, I contacted your mortgage company and obtained current figures on your principal balance and the amount accrued in your escrow account. This is your current principal balance after the May 1st payment."

(Get permission, the loan number, and loan company from the owner during the measure-up appointment.)

Estimated interest on current mortgage

"Although not commonly known, a house payment differs from a rent payment in that it is paid in arrears. This means the payment you made on May 1st covers the interest due on your loan for the month of April. This is the way virtually all mortgage interest is calculated.

"This means, starting with the first day of each month, a homeowner owes the mortgage company one-day's interest on the principal balance for each day of the month starting the 1st. Of course, we don't know the day of the month the closing of your house is going to be held, so I included approximately one-month's interest in your estimated expenses. Depending on when the sales will close, this figure will range between one-day's interest and a full-month's interest, as indicated on this estimate sheet."

Record release of present mortgage

"Your current mortgage is recorded at the courthouse for the protection of your present loan company. It must be released at the time of sale. The fee for this is based on the number of pages the mortgage is long. The cost will be approximately _____ dollars."

Prepayment fee on current mortgage

"Under the terms of your current mortgage, you will owe your loan company a prepayment fee if your current loan is paid off at this time. This will be one (two, three) percent of your current balance.

"There is a possibility of getting this waived by placing the buyer's new loan at the company that holds your current mortgage. This may or may not be to your advantage. If your property is sold with FHA or VA terms, we may be able to obtain a larger net for you by placing the new loan at a different company charging a lower discount rate."

"At the time we receive a purchase agreement on your house, I will research all the financing options available to find the best arrangement possible at that time. Of course, I will prepare a new estimate sheet reflecting the lowest financing charges available to you then.

"All available options will be explained to you when a purchase agreement is received. You can then make the decisions on which options to take."

Escrow adjustment

"Your current mortgage company is escrowing $135 per month for tax and insurance payments. The account normally has a surplus of funds because the loan company must collect enough money in advance to be able to pay tax assessments and insurance premiums when they come due. This money will be refunded to you at the time of closing."

Property tax adjustment

"Local property taxes are paid twice a year. Taxes for the first half of the year (starting January 1st) are not due and payable until April 1st. Because of this, you will be in arrears or will have paid taxes in advance on any particular date. These taxes will be prorated at the time of closing.

"If in arrears, the amount owed, on a prorated basis, will be deducted from your net and credited to the buyer. If your taxes are prepaid at the time of closing, the buyer will refund to you the amount due on the daily prorated basis. You will pay taxes only for the time you actually own the house.

"Although the figures for your escrow refund and tax proration will change, your total net will remain approximately the same. This is because changes in the tax proration will be offset by the deposit made to your escrow account with every house payment you make."

Taxes are paid differently in different parts of the country. Adjust this explanation to your locale.

Brokerage Fee

"The real estate fee for selling your property is seven percent of the final sales price. This is due if a buyer for your property is found as outlined in the listing agreement.

I will explain in detail what we do for this fee in a few moments."

Avoid discussing the commission at this point. If the sellers have any real questions or objections, they will surface when you explain the terms of the listing agreement to them. Explaining your marketing program in depth will frequently preclude any further questions or attempts to get you to reduce your commission.

Title insurance

"The use of title insurance has replaced the use of abstracts in residential real estate sales in most cases. It insures that the buyer is receiving a clear title. The fee for this service is normally split equally between the buyer and seller."

(Your local practice may differ.)

"The same companies that performed abstract work in the past now issue insurance policies guaranteeing a valid, marketable title to the buyer. These companies research the local courthouse records and prepare a binder informing the salespersons, buyers, and sellers what needs to be done to convey clear title.

"This binder will tell us what legal documents we will need to prepare to convey the title. Included will be what type of deeds will be required and how they need to be prepared. Other requirements, such as lien waivers and possibly releases for different types of encumbrances, will be included."

Discount points

"Fixed-rate FHA and VA mortgages offer advantages in addition to interest rates that are normally lower than fixed-rate conventional mortgages. All FHA and VA mortgages are assumable by any buyer the seller approves."

Explain to the client the need to obtain a release of liability when selling a property on a loan assumption basis (*see* Chapter 3, "Direct-Mail Prospecting").

"In addition, the lender is allowed to charge only a nominal assumption fee. With few exceptions, the interest rate is guaranteed to stay the same for the life of the loan."

As of this writing, FHA adjustable rate mortgages are the only exception.

> "There is never a prepayment fee on these mortgages. On top of all this, a minimal or no down payment is required. For these reasons, FHA and VA loans are very attractive to buyers. In fact current statistics show that 53 percent of all house purchases financed with new loans in this area are sold with new FHA or VA loans."

Check your MLS final sold records to determine the percentage in your area.

> "Unless sellers have a low-interest, low-equity assumable loan on their property, they eliminate almost two-thirds of the valid buying prospects for their house when not offering FHA and VA terms. For all of these reasons, I recommend you offer FHA and VA terms when marketing your property."

If they object to paying points, use the "discount explanation sheet" covered in Chapter 6, "Preparing the Listing Presentation." Include comments something like this:

> "Mr. and Mrs. Seller, I understand how you feel about paying discount points, but as I've mentioned, most of the cost of points is brought back to sellers in the form of higher sales prices in most sales in which they are paid by the seller. Plus, if you don't offer FHA and VA terms, you are eliminating approximately half of the prospective buyers for your house. That, in essence, means it will take twice as long to sell it."

Company and personal promotional material

> "I've included some material telling you a little about myself and the company I work for. I've been in residential sales for over ten years, having sold over 320 homes in that period. Helping people with their real estate needs is my full-time business. The company I am affiliated with sells the most real estate of any agency in the city. Last year, our company took part in 43 percent of the residential sales in the metropolitan area."

Most prospective sellers are not interested in more than a brief summary of your past accomplishments. Keep it brief, just long enough to establish your credibility. The thrust of the entire presentation should be aimed at what you will be doing for the prospect directly. Avoid using this part of the presentation to stroke your own ego. Keep the information to one page each for yourself and your company. A company brochure summarizing its strong points is helpful.

PRESENTING YOUR MARKETING PROGRAM

The next major portion of the presentation consists of your marketing program for the seller's property. Introduce it as follows:

> "Mr. and Mrs. Seller, a lot of salespersons think that placing your property in the multiple-listing book and running a few ads is a good effort in trying to sell it. I disagree. For seven percent of the sales price, you deserve a salesperson who really works hard and makes every reasonable effort to get the most out of your property as quickly as possible.
>
> "These are the different ways in which I will promote your house to the public and to other real estate salespersons. How I promote your property is important because the chance of my finding the buyer for your house is only about one in ten. What I do to promote your property to the public and to other salespersons is what will get it sold. The first promotional program I am going to explain is one that has proved over the years to be very effective in generating buying prospects."

Sample "Open House" Brochures

Give each prospect a sample "open house" brochure and say:

> "This program consists of mailing 200 open-house notices through your immediate neighborhood. Each brochure will have a photo and description of your house as well as an invitation to the open house. Many sellers ask why I mail the brochures in the immediate neighborhood, as most people living in the neighborhood own their own homes. This is true in your neighborhood, as there are few rentals. However, studies have shown and my experience has supported the fact that often when a buyer wants to move into

an area, he or she has a friend or relative already living there.

"Actually, the people who live in your neighborhood probably know more buying prospects for your house than any real estate professional in the city. Being located where you are, probably only one out of ten people who live in this subdivision will see your 'for sale' sign. By mailing brochures throughout the entire neighborhood, we are directing our advertising dollars to a group of people very likely to know potential buyers for your house.

"I have found this program to be more effective than newspaper advertising for generating buyers. Newspaper ads generate many phone calls from prospective buyers but these prospects rarely buy the house they called about. I have found that I can find more actual buyers for a house I am trying to sell by using this 'open house' brochure program than by newspaper advertising. This is very important as we have a limited amount of money we can spend advertising your house and we want to make the most of it."

Let them look over the sample brochures briefly and then distribute an open-house brochure you have prepared in advance on their house.

"I have prepared a brochure on your house. Could you please take a few minutes to look it over and let me know what you think of it? I would appreciate any suggestions you may have for improving it."

Let them look over the brochure. If you have done a good job on it, they usually will say it is great. If they have any suggestions for improvements, note them on your copy of the sample brochure and say:

"That would be a significant improvement. I will have my secretary make the changes you suggested."

Now bring out your appointment book and open it to a premarked page.

"My secretary could have this mailing prepared and mailed in time for an open house on September 1st. Would that suit your schedule?"

If they agree to an open house on that day, write the open house starting and finishing time in your appointment book on the page for September 1st. You can suggest they make a notation of the time and date on their kitchen calendar if it is in sight. At this point, you have the listing and you have not even shown them the listing agreement. Adjust the date if necessary but get a commitment if at all possible and write it down. Let them see you write a note to your secretary asking him or her to make any suggested changes the sellers desired in the brochure and specifying the date the mailing needs to be taken to the post office.

After using dozens of different approaches during hundreds of listing presentations, I have found the preceding to be the most powerful, effective trial close possible when listing residential properties. This technique alone will dramatically increase the number of listings you obtain immediately after you put it into use.

Sample Salesperson Brochures

"This is the current issue of the local multiple-listing book. There are approximately 3,500 houses for sale in this issue. I can guarantee you that no salesperson in this city goes through every page of this book each week to see what is new on the market. For that reason, I prepared another brochure designed specifically for real estate salespersons.

"This brings your house to the attention of another group of people likely to know potential buyers. Any salesperson receiving a brochure who has a buyer looking for a house in the same price range and neighborhood as yours will either make an appointment to show it or call for additional information.

"By distributing brochures to the people in your neighborhood and to real estate persons active in this area, we are directing advertising dollars to two groups of people very likely to help find a buyer."

Use success stories for the above two approaches as soon as you have them to tell.

Samples of Other Regularly Used Advertising

"These are samples of other forms of ads that will be used to promote your house. Your house will be advertised in a local advertising supplement every third week with a photo and brief description of your house. We have found the photo ads to bring a higher response rate than classified ads."

Adapt this to include any specific advertising approaches you plan to use, specifying the frequency with which they will run. This lets sellers know what to expect in the way their house will be advertised throughout the initial marketing period.

"Thanks for Showing My Listing" Form

Distribute samples and say:

"Mr. and Mrs. Seller, as we discussed earlier, buyers now active in the market will determine the desirability and market value of your house. For that reason, it is important to get as much feedback as possible from every potential buyer who looks at your property, whether he or she is or is not interested in buying it.

"To obtain this information, I will mail a showing evaluation form to every salesperson who shows your house. Included with the evaluation form will be a stamped, addressed return envelope.

"This form asks the opinion of both the showing salesperson and the buying prospect regarding the market value of the house. It also asks the salesperson if there were any aspects of the property that generated a negative reaction in the buyer's eyes. It goes on to ask for suggestions on how to make the property more desirable to buyers. This approach is more effective than merely calling the showing salesperson for an oral opinion.

"All feedback we receive, positive or negative, is valuable. It will give us the pulse of the marketplace, allowing us to adjust our marketing approach to generate the maximum showing traffic possible. Many times buyers will pick up on small things that you and I could miss. This lets us know what the buyers are thinking, and the more we see your property through a typical buyer's eyes, the sooner it will sell.

"I will forward all evaluation forms to you as soon as I receive them. If you have any questions about them, please call me. If not, we will discuss them in detail during one of our periodic visits during the marketing period."

Proposed Marketing Schedule

When finished with the "Thanks for Showing My Listing" form, distribute copies of the proposed marketing schedule. Briefly go over every entry. Little explanation will be necessary, as you have already discussed in detail the promotional programs you will use when marketing the house.

The reason for consolidating the plan on one sheet of paper is to provide you with additional trial closing opportunities. Be liberal in your use of tie-downs.

> "Will a tour of your house by our salespersons on August 10 fit into your schedule?"

Obtain a consensus on the proposed dates, changing any that conflict with the seller's schedule.

THE LISTING AGREEMENT

The listing agreement should be presented using a relaxed approach and at the same tempo and tone at which you have been working. When discussing the listing agreement, be at least as relaxed as at any other time in the presentation. Presenting the market analysis in the order outlined provides a natural flow leading to a discussion of the listing agreement. Introduce it in this manner:

> "Mr. and Mrs. Seller, this is the agreement that allows us to market your house. There are a lot of misconceptions about what this agreement does and I would like to discuss a few of them. This is not an agreement to sell your house. It is merely an employment contract under which you are hiring me and the agency I work for to represent you in the sale of your house. It is a contingency agreement under which you pay for our services only if we perform our duties as outlined.
>
> "This agreement is between you and the agency. It allows us to place your house on the market and outlines the terms under which you are offering your property for sale. The agreement you reach with the eventual buyer may be different in many respects than what is outlined in the listing. The terms specified in the listing are the conditions you state as being acceptable terms of sale. A potential buyer is not limited to these terms when submitting an actual purchase agreement. A prospective buyer has the right to make any offer he or she desires.
>
> "You have three options when receiving an offer to purchase with a price or terms different than those at which

you listed the house. You may accept the offer, reject it outright, or propose a counteroffer. Countering the original offer makes it void.

"The way your agreement with my broker and myself is structured, you will owe a fee only if we find a ready, willing, and able buyer under the listed price and terms or any other price or terms you find acceptable. In all other instances, you will not owe the agency a cent for any services rendered or for any money spent on advertising and promotion.

"I would like to take a few minutes to explain the agreement, paragraph by paragraph. Please stop me any time you have a question."

Explain the listing agreement without reading it. Explaining it in everyday language eliminates a lot of the natural fear of the agreement the average homeowner has. Take your time and answer any questions large or small, moving (as usual) at the homeowner's speed. Check with your managing broker to see if your company has specific policies on how to explain the listing agreement.

Here is a suggested approach to use when covering portions of the listing agreement that many salespersons find difficult to explain to their prospects:

1. Length of Agreement

"This allows us to market your property for 120 days starting today. Sellers often ask why it needs to be placed on the market for what seems like a long time. This gives me and the agency I work for adequate time to produce a sale giving you the highest net possible. Of course, if you have a change in plans, and decide not to sell at this time, you can take your house off the market and we will change the expiration date to accommodate you."

At times a seller will continue to object to the length of the agreement. In cases like this it is best to incorporate a termination clause rather than shorten the term of the agreement. This should be used only when necessary. You may have to obtain approval from your manager before doing this on a regular basis. Approach it as follows:

"Mr. and Mrs. Seller, I understand your concern. Would you feel better if I added a clause stating that, at your discretion, you can terminate this listing agreement at any time with a one-day written notice if you are not satisfied with the service I give you?"

In reality you are not giving anything away. If they are that unhappy with you, you would probably terminate your relationship with them anyhow. Be sure they understand that this will not allow them to sell the property directly to a buyer the agency has produced to avoid paying a commission. This is a delicate area and you should not make this point when discussing the termination clause. The sellers will become aware of this when you discuss the paragraph outlining the protection period the agency has following the termination date of the agreement. Try something like this when explaining the protection clause:

> "This paragraph states that if the house is sold to a buyer generated through the agency's efforts within 180 days of the expiration date of the listing, you will owe the company the agreed-upon fee. Of course, I understand you would never do this, but it is our company policy to include this clause in every property we place on the market. I hope you understand."

State this casually as just another part of the agreement and drop it.

I have used a termination clause for years and have yet to have a seller make a serious attempt at using it to avoid paying a commission rightfully owed. Develop exact wording acceptable to your manager and use this when necessary to obtain a listing for the number of marketing days you, the salesperson, desire.

2. Price   This should be agreed upon long before you get to the listing agreement. If it is not resolved yet or, as happens in many cases, the prospect wants to reopen discussion, be patient. Work with the seller to get the property listed at the best price possible. Refer to the earlier part of this chapter for suggested approaches.

3. What If I Find a Buyer on My Own?

> "Mr. and Mrs. Seller, this agreement gives the agency I work for the exclusive right to act as your agent for the term of the agreement. That means that a fee will be owed if the

eventual buyer of the house is found during that period. However, if you have a specific person you feel may buy the property, we can exlude him or her from the agreement. This means you will not owe a real estate fee to the agency for any sale to that party."

Most sellers understand the necessity for this clause in the agreement and ask mainly out of curiosity. Note: This will not apply if using other than an exclusive-right-to-sell listing.

4. Will You Negotiate Your Fee?

"Good question! I understand your motivations. If I were you, I would ask it, too. As I am sure you know, the fee a real estate agency charges for its services is negotiable. However, I personally will not accept a listing at less than our normal fee. Please let me explain.

"If I list your property at a commission rate less than that specified by my broker, any reduction I negotiate will come out of my part of the fee. In plain words, if I list your house at a reduced commission, the amount of the reduction comes directly out of my paycheck.

"I provide what I think is superior service. I feel that the direct-mail promotions, brochures promoting your house to other salespersons, photo ads, and other tools that I use are necessary to sell your house for top dollar in the shortest possible time. These all cost money and in many instances are expenses other salespersons avoid.

"I am sure that with very little effort you could find another salesperson willing to list your house for less. However, I feel you get what you pay for. Salespersons who list properties at a lower rate either provide fewer services or are not good enough at their profession to get business without discounting their price.

"The amount a real estate agency can charge for its fee is another function of the marketplace. Please understand my position, and I will understand yours if you feel the need to work with a salesperson who will list your house for less."

Be flexible during your presentation. Remain in control while adapting the pace and contents to the prospect's particular needs as they become apparent. Most objections are posed because the salesperson did not address the seller's initial concerns and questions fully during the presentation. Make it a habit to anticipate and diffuse the objections before you get to the listing agreement.

After explaining the agreement, merely sign the agreement as the listing salesperson, mark two 'X's where the sellers are to sign, and turn it around. If the presentation was done correctly, meaning all objections and questions were handled in full, the signature is almost automatic.

Constructively critique every listing presentation you make as soon as you have completed it. Revise it, update it, and improve it to make yourself a winner in the presentation game.

CHAPTER 8

OBTAINING PRICE, TERMS, AND CONDITION ADJUSTMENTS

You list a house and do everything but stand on your head to get it sold, only to end up with an expired listing. Worse still, it seems every time this happens the owner immediately lists with a competitor, drops the price $4,000, and the house sells in two weeks! I call this the heartbreak of expired listings. Expired listings can be avoided by listing the property "right" in the first place, meaning at a salable price, terms, and condition, and making adjustments in price, terms, or condition if called for by the marketplace.

All salespersons try to list properties "right" when they initially are put on the market. It is not always possible. Often the seller refuses to take a salesperson's marketing advice and demands the agent "try at a higher price" or "see how it goes without doing the repairs." Sometimes salespersons recommend an overly optimistic price in a legitimate effort to get as much money as possible for the seller. Any salesperson who lists a respectable amount of property takes listings that turn out to be unsalable at the listed price and terms. In these cases the salesperson must determine why the property has not sold and then obtain adjustments throughout the marketing period until the property is sold.

EDUCATING THE SELLER

Getting sellers to market their property correctly is accomplished by educating them on how the marketplace works and how the marketing of property must be tailored to current market conditions. The following explains a logical sequence you can use when working with sellers to get their property sold as quickly as possible at the highest price the market will yield.

At the Listing Presentation

You set the stage for future adjustments, if they become necessary, during the initial presentation as outlined in Chapter 7, "Getting the Listing." The points you should stress during the listing presentation and throughout the marketing period are:

1. Property values are not determined by sellers and/or salespersons. For the most part they are determined by the buyers currently active in the marketplace.
2. Even though sellers do not determine the value of their property, they determine how fast it sells by what they price it at, the condition they have it in, and the financing terms they offer to prospective buyers.
3. If a property does not sell, it is because, based on its location, condition, and offering terms, the price is too high.

The next step in your journey to getting the property sold is to explain what you will be doing during the first five weeks on the market to generate a buyer. This does two things. It eliminates questions from the seller during the initial marketing period about what you are doing to sell the house. The second thing it does is set the stage for adjustments. You can use an approach something like this when presenting the proposed marketing schedule:

> "Mr. and Mrs. Seller, I understand that I am listing your house for 120 days and have explained only what I will be doing to sell it for the next five weeks. That is because by the end of five weeks we will have enough feedback from prospective buyers and their salespersons to determine how the marketplace is reacting to our marketing efforts and asking price. This will guide us in deciding how we should

market the property in the following five weeks to maximize our chances for a sale during that time.

The third thing to do at the 'listing presentation is to encourage the sellers to call whenever their house is being shown and whenever they have a worry or concern, no matter how small. We ask them to call when the property is being shown so that we can contact the salesperson showing the property and provide him or her with whatever information or assistance we can to help put a sale together. This is frequently helpful for the showing salesperson because, although they should, many salespersons do not preview a listing before showing it. Often a property will be shown by a newer salesperson who needs moral support or technical assistance in order to make the sale work. Consider educating and assisting newer salespersons who have buying prospects on your listings as part of the job of representing the seller.

If possible, talk to the salesperson showing your listing before the actual showing takes place. This gives you a chance to tell him or her about any recent adjustments in price, terms, or condition and to build up interest in the property. Generating interest by being enthusiastic about your listings and expressing a desire to work with selling salespersons often motivates them to sell your listing rather than someone else's.

Encouraging your sellers to call you every time they feel the need to talk to you should be stressed frequently. A seller's most minor concern can grow into a full-fledged problem if the salesperson is unaware of it. Avoid or minimize problems by regularly letting your sellers know you are open to their questions and worries. This keeps small problems from becoming big ones.

During the Marketing Period

Prospects who have viewed the property and salespersons who have shown it are the primary sources for determining why a property is not selling. We can obtain their opinions in several areas and use them to inform our sellers and better market the property.

Tour feedback

When touring listings many companies have the touring salespersons give their estimates of the property's market value and make suggestions for improving the salability of the properties on tour. If your company does not have salespersons complete written evaluations of the properties toured, solicit the opinions of three or four salespersons who toured the property, put the comments in written form, and forward them to the seller. This gives the seller, during the first few weeks on the market, an idea of how real estate salespersons currently active in the field view their property and can be especially helpful if your seller insisted on overpricing the property.

Open house feedback

A simple but effective technique consists of taking notes immediately after the property has been visited by a buying prospect. After the first visitor leaves, take a tablet, write down "couple number one," and record the comments which they made about the house. These should include all positive and negative comments and any opinions offered on the asking price or market value of the property. Continue to record all significant comments from all visitors throughout the open house. Use a carbon and leave a copy at the house before you leave. Mail a copy to the sellers if they have already moved.

"Thanks for showing my listing" form

This form gives you the most usable feedback possible from salespersons who have shown your listings. It provides more detailed information than you normally get in a phone conversation and it gives you something tangible to show your sellers. When you receive a completed evaluation, make copies for your file and mail or drop off the original to your seller. If you choose to not use the "Thanks For Showing My Listing" form, telephone all salespersons who show your listings to get feedback. Take notes, again make copies, and forward them to the seller.

Showing feedback

Take notes whenever you show the property yourself. Telephone your customer and relay the results immediately following each showing. Add the notes to your file and review them in the presence of your seller during any visit to review market activity or present an offer.

Marketplace feedback summary

By continually collecting opinions from salespersons and prospective buyers and forwarding them to sellers, we educate them on how prospective buyers are viewing their property. They may be hurt and offended when they receive a "Thanks for Showing My Listing" form in the mail that contains serious criticisms about their house but it is an effective way to get them to start viewing their property more objectively. In this way you prepare them for the fact that changes may be needed. Continually monitoring the pulse of the marketplace gives you a basis to determine why the property has not sold.

WHY THE PROPERTY HAS NOT SOLD

Frequently houses do not sell as fast as the seller or salesperson would like. This occurs even in instances where the seller and salesperson thought the property was listed right and promoted aggressively. When a parcel of real estate does not sell, without a doubt the marketplace has determined that the price is too high. Location, condition, and offering terms enter into the equation but they are all a function of price. The following describes how each affects true market value and salability.

Curable Condition Problems

Properties with condition problems fall into one of two categories—curable or incurable. With luck the property you are trying to list will have only curable defects. These can be corrected with a scrub brush, paint brush, tools, and some money. Properties that sparkle and shine sell best in all market conditions, good or poor. During soft markets, houses in top condition are frequently the only ones that do sell at a price favorable to the seller. Homeowners do not understand the extent to which this is true. You must explain it to them.

The market value of a house is based on its present condition. A property's potential rarely puts anything tangible in a seller's pocket. If a property needs work, the salesperson has a responsibility to make the seller aware of what needs to be done and to make sure the work is completed. An FHA or VA preappraisal can be helpful in these instances.

Do your best to have these condition problems resolved before the property goes on the market. Often sellers will not make these and other types of improvements until the marketplace says: "We're not interested!" The best way to focus attention on needed improvements is to use the opinions of prospective buyers who viewed the house as a basis for discussion on what improvements should be made and how best to do them.

If the sellers are going to do the work themselves, obtain a commitment as to when it will be completed. Asking to have the work done by the open house date is a logical and effective approach. Many times the sellers will be unable to do the work or may choose not to do it themselves. Develop a list of tradesmen and handymen capable of doing the most commonly needed home repairs. Whenever possible refer two or more people capable of doing the work to the sellers. The sellers can then obtain more than one bid, helping ensure a good job at at reasonable price. Build your portfolio of reliable contractors and be loyal to them. In return, any work you refer to them will be done quickly and at a competitive price.

Another type of condition problem is "dirty-house syndrome." The sellers do not think it is dirty. If they did, they would clean it up. In most of these cases the sellers think the house looks fine. The sellers should be convinced to get and keep the house brilliantly clean the entire time the house is on the market. To ensure a quick sale at top dollar, a house should be immaculate. Get your sellers to pay attention to the little things; they are important to buyers. The stove should be spotless; walls, floors, and carpets cleaned if necessary; shower stalls scoured; trash in the alley hauled away, and so on. All light bulbs and switches need to be in working order. The garage and utility room should be orderly. All this makes a positive impression on buyers and is worth doing.

A gentle reminder when you list the property about the importance of a clean house is often all that is needed. If a problem remains after one or two weeks on the market, give the problem additional attention. Try the following. A day or two after the salespersons' tour, meet with the owners. Tell them that the salespeople who viewed it felt the general condition of the house would discourage any buying prospects they may have for it. This will be a reiteration of what you told your sellers at the time you listed the property.

Give the sellers a written list of specific suggestions made by other salespersons. If necessary, ask your fellow salespersons for constructive criticism following the tour. This takes the heat off you and illustrates the need for improvement to your sellers.

After you have been on the market for a period of time, you can also use the "Thanks For Showing My Listing" form to combat dirty-house syndrome.

Some salespersons suggest having a specific list of tasks done by a professional cleaning service if the sellers are unwilling or unable to complete the tasks themselves. Carpet cleaning, deodorizing, and window-washing are typical of the tasks sellers are unlikely to want to do themselves. Continue to work with your sellers on "dirty-house syndrome" until the problems are corrected.

Vacant houses pose a special problem. Emptying a house of furniture, pictures, wall hangings, window coverings, etc., highlights every little spot, stain, and smudge. When selling vacant houses, a superior cleaning job is a must. If they already have moved out, get the sellers' permission to have the house professionally cleaned. Even if they still live in town, owners find it difficult to go back to the house they once lived in and clean it for someone else more thoroughly than they ever did for themselves. Get to know a reliable cleaning person or company. Work closely with them to get the house in the condition you want. This approach puts the property on the market in the best condition possible.

Sellers who are reluctant to get their house in shape need to be educated to the harsh realities of the market. They do not understand that a reduction in market value of $4,000 or more can result from $1,000 worth of needed paint, repairs, and cleaning. In addition to the price penalty, condition problems can add weeks and months to the time it takes to sell a property. Educate your sellers. Follow the lead of corporate buy-out companies. When they have a vacant house to sell, they immediately clean, paint, and shampoo or replace carpet.

Incurable Condition Defects

Incurable condition defects present another difficult problem. They cannot be solved with a reasonable amount of money and effort. Examples are unusually steep driveways or eight-foot retaining walls. Cutting the price to compensate is the only solution. That is basic marketing. It is best to do this at the time the property is listed, but at times sellers will not acknowledge the problem until the property is listed and the marketplace has shown no interest.

Most sellers are reluctant to accept the fact that they have a problem. The defect, whatever it is, is no surprise to them. They have lived with it for years, probably learned to laugh about it and learned, too, to love the house in spite of it. Whatever the defect, they will defend against the idea that it is something that reduces the property value of their home because they have learned to live with it. Make sure that the sellers understand that it is both their responsibility and yours as salesperson to make full disclosure of any latent defects.

Reducing the price because of a defect of this type is a tough task for a salesperson. But it often can be resolved if you use the following tack:

> "Mr. and Mrs. Seller, I would like you to think back to when you bought this property. You felt you got a good buy, didn't you? Of course you did, otherwise you wouldn't have bought it. Speaking frankly, one of the reasons you got such a good buy is because of the steep driveway. It was reflected in the price. You will have to recognize that fact and compensate for it when pricing your property for sale."

A good rule of thumb is: **If you buy at a discount because of an incurable defect, you will have to sell at a discount or you will have difficulties in producing a timely sale.** The amount the market value is discounted varies with the extent of the problem. Based on research done on comparables, proceed to obtain an adjustment.

In summary, if the marketplace has told you the property has not sold because of a condition problem, it must be corrected. If curable, you have a choice: Repair the defect or reduce the price. If incurable, the house must be priced lower to reflect that fact, or it will not sell.

Location

"Location, location, location." We have often heard that these are the three most important factors in determining what property is worth. It is true. Buyers pay a premium for excellent location. Conversely, poor location depresses the market value of a property.

Poor location can come in two forms. The first is an areawide problem. A property can be located in a seedy, rundown, or otherwise undesirable area or neighborhood. All property prices in the immediate area are depressed. The second type of location problem is when the property is located adjacent to or near an undesirable structure or physical landmark. Examples are properties on a busy street, across the alley from a smelly industrial plant, or backed up to a busy set of railroad tracks. These properties sell for less than similar properties in the same neighborhood that are not located immediately next to a marketplace liability.

What makes location defects difficult to resolve is that most sellers have warm memories and thoughts of comfort and dignity when they reflect on the years they have spent in the house. They are seldom willing or able to accept the fact that their property is worth less because of a location they learned to accept long ago. They are blind to the problem. The longer they have lived there, the tougher the salesperson's task. The best solution is again to rely on comparable sales to establish and illustrate the extent of the problem. The only remedy for a poorly located property is attractive pricing and terms. Again, educate your seller.

Financing

Experienced professionals know that prospects do not buy houses based on price alone. They shop and buy payments. Arrangements that provide for a lower payment generally translate into a higher sales price and greater net to the seller. In addition to possibly raising the seller's net, favorable terms also can be used in many cases to overcome location or condition defects, inspiring faster sales for many properties.

Financing can be used to make a property more attractive to buyers in a number of ways. One of the best is for the seller to offer FHA and VA terms. These loans generally require a smaller down payment and provide for a lower interest rate and monthly payment than most fixed-rate conventional loans. Other available options include variable rate mortgages, graduated payment mortgages, buydowns, seller carrybacks, contracts for deed, and wrap mortgages; the list is almost endless.

Available financing options are in a constant state of flux with different options being more or less attractive at different times. You need to be well versed in what types of financing are available and how each type works. With this knowledge you can educate sellers to what financing should be offered to help sell their property quickly with the least cost and most benefit to them. If the property has not sold and you have determined that unattractive financing terms are the culprit, you have two choices: Sweeten the terms for the buyers or reduce the price to compensate.

SIX DEADLY ERRORS

Many salespersons unintentionally commit acts that keep their listings from selling. They, with the consent of their sellers, commit one or more of the following classic errors:

Unrealistic pricing—Many salespersons "buy listings," placing a house on the market at too high a price in order to obtain the listing. The salesperson either is desperate to get any kind of listing or has not done his or her homework. Whatever the cause, hinting at the possibility of a sale at an unrealistically high price is an easy first step toward an expired listing.

Promoting unrealistic expectations—Usually it is the promise of a quick sale or an unusual amount of showing traffic. Some salespersons will tell sellers, "I have a buyer for your house." Such promises are often broken, and broken promises weaken relationships. A professional in our business does not make promises he or she cannot keep.

Failure to identify defects—Sellers in most cases think their property looks fine. If they did not, they would have changed it. Failing to open their eyes to problems that are killing sales is a good way to kill relationships.

Ignoring the competition—Not keeping your sellers up-to-date on comparable properties for sale in their area creates another obstacle to correct pricing. Neglecting current market conditions as they change during the marketing period hinders successful marketing and breeds resentment.

Not using financing as a marketing tool—Failing to educate your sellers to financing options they could offer to increase the salability of their property is unacceptable and the mark of a substandard salesperson.

Failure to emphasize the importance of price—Price, price, price. As mentioned before, price is the single most important factor an owner has control over in determining the marketability of the property. Not hammering this point home to your sellers when the property is listed and during the marketing period sows the seed for expired listings more than any other single reason.

Any one of these errors on the listing salesperson's part can strain a relationship. It may leave an overpriced or poorly marketed property stranded on the market, resulting in an expired listing and an unearned commission. Avoid these potential pitfalls by working closely with your sellers during the marketing period to make adjustments in price, terms, or condition when called for by the marketplace.

OBTAINING ADJUSTMENTS

There are three optimum times during the marketing period in which to obtain adjustments in price, terms, and condition. They are: (1) after the initial marketing period, (2) when you receive a concerned call from a seller regarding lack of market activity, and (3) after you receive a low offer. We will look at each of these.

After the Initial Marketing Period

This is an excellent time to review progress and obtain adjustments if you set the stage correctly during the listing presentation. This should be four to six weeks after the property is listed (*see* Chapter 7).

When You Receive a Concerned Call

A second opportune time to get adjustments is when your customer calls, unhappy and wondering why his or her house has not sold. Many times these calls indicate the sellers are seeking your help, as they want to take whatever action is appropriate to get the property sold but do not really know what to do. In some cases the sellers' motivation has changed and for the first time they are ready to get serious about marketing the property correctly.

The following is one of the best ways to turn a seller complaint call into sale-producing action. When an upset seller calls, share his or her concern. Listen. Listen closely and understand how he or she feels. Do not interrupt. You do not have to agree, just listen. You should talk only after the seller has finished expressing his or her thoughts. You can then agree that progress to date has been unsatisfactory. After all, the house is not sold. Make an appointment to see the sellers in person to discuss what can be done. Prepare an "adjustment package" as outlined later in this chapter and present it to your sellers. Adjustments obtained this way turn your sellers' unrest into something positive that will help sell their house.

After Low Offers Are Received

Overpricing is almost always the cause if you are consistently receiving low ball offers on one of your listings. When your seller angrily rejects yet another ridiculous offer, let the anger roll off your shoulders and avoid reacting emotionally. In most instances the seller's anger is not personally directed toward you. The seller is mad at the whole world because the house has not sold. Convert the anger into something positive. Use it to obtain an adjustment if it is called for. Approach it like this:

"Mr. Seller, I understand your being upset over another low offer. But experience tells us that if you do not change the way in which you are marketing your house, those will most likely be the only kind of offers we will be getting. Time and time again, the marketplace has shown that the closer a property is priced to its true market value, the closer the offers will be to the asking price. Let me give you an example: If a house is worth $80,000 and the owner prices it at $90,000, the offers often come in around $70,000. Buyers underbid what they think the true market value is by the amount they feel the property is overpriced. The fact that we continue to receive low offers is a strong indicator that the buyers in the marketplace at this time think your price is significantly higher than it should be. We need to recognize the signal the marketplace is sending us and compensate for it, or the property will likely go unsold."

All three of the above situations give you, the salesperson, an excellent opening to make an appointment for and obtain an adjustment in price.

PREPARING FOR THE ADJUSTMENT APPOINTMENT

Prepare for meeting the sellers by updating your market analysis. Compile all final sales, pendings, expireds, and new listings that have entered the system since you prepared the original analysis. Next gather and consolidate all comments and feedback collected from salespersons and buying prospects who have viewed the property. Summarize all efforts made to promote the property. Include copies of all classified ads, open house brochures, promotional material distributed to salespersons, multiple-listing data sheets, etc. The final inserts will be a list of written suggestions you feel will help sell the property and a form upon which the seller can authorize adjustments. This packet will form the basis for deciding how to market the property over the next month to six weeks.

Make an appointment with your sellers, allowing ample time for an in-depth discussion. You may need the time to explain the importance of responding to what the marketplace is telling them. An excellent way to start the appointment is to ask your sellers to help you complete the "Five-Week Results Review" (Example 24). Completing this simple test only takes five or ten minutes, yet gives you and your sellers a chance to focus on possible reasons the property has not sold and to decide if an adjustment is called for.

Present and discuss the materials you have prepared. When your sellers' questions have been answered, suggest the changes you feel are needed to get the property sold. If price is the problem, prepare and include a seller's estimated net sheet at the price and terms you want the sellers to agree to. If you want a $3,000 adjustment, you might prepare net sheets based on adjustments of $4,000 and $3,000. Try for a larger adjustment than you want and negotiate. This approach is less arbitrary than suggesting one price and arguing over it. If improvements of the property are needed, prepare a detailed list so your sellers know exactly what you want.

Put all suggestions for adjustments in written form. Make copies for your sellers and yourself. Do not be afraid to tell the sellers they need to make adjustments and do not be afraid to ask for what you feel is necessary. If you do not, you are not doing the job you were hired for: getting the property sold.

Responding to market conditions by making adjustments in price, terms, and condition is essential to producing a timely sale at the top of the fair range. If market response is poor, identify and remedy the causes. Above all, the sellers must be convinced that price—the proper price—is the prime factor.

Example 24

THE FIVE WEEK RESULT PLAN

This self-test was designed for the use of real estate listing salespersons and/or owners of properties for sale. Its purpose is to help the salesperson or owners more clearly focus on how the marketplace is responding to the combined marketing efforts of the owners and their salesperson. It serves as a guide to whether an adjustment in price, terms, or condition are called for.

	Yes	No
Has a written offer been received on the property in the last five weeks?	___	___
Has there be an adjustmnet of five percent or more in the listing price in the last five weeks?	___	___
Has the condition of the property been improved significantly in the last five weeks?	___	___
Have offering terms more attractive to potential buyers been added in the last five weeks?	___	___
Is there a qualified buying prospect interested in the property at the present time?	___	___

Four or five "No" answers strongly indicate that a change in marketing strategy will be necessary to produce a sale. The basic options of every seller are to adjust the price, add more favorable terms, or improve the condition of the property. Keep in mind that location, condition, and offering terms are all a function of price. Market studies have shown that if market activity is unproductive for a period of five weeks, it is unlikely that a sale will occur in the next five weeks unless an adjustment in price, terms, or condition are made.

PART IV
NEGOTIATING AND CLOSING THE SALE

CHAPTER 9

NEGOTIATING THE AGREEMENT

Negotiating agreements is easy after you learn to focus on the elements of the agreement instead of on the personalities of the people involved. Of course personalities have to be taken into consideration whenever you are dealing with people but they should not be the focus of the negotiations.

Another important factor in winning the negotiation game is keeping things in perspective while others are upset or even hysterical. As Mark McCormack says in his excellent book, *What They Don't Teach You in Harvard Business School,* "Act, don't react." Acting rationally and keeping personal feelings separate from the issues makes the salesperson more effective in all phases of negotiation. Considering all areas as potentially negotiable and making every effort to understand the viewpoint of all parties allow structuring the best possible compromise for everyone. We will go through the steps involved in correctly presenting an offer to purchase.

MAKING THE APPOINTMENT

Unless working with out-of-town sellers, *never* discuss details about any purchase agreement over the telephone. Written agreements should be discussed only when face-to-face with your customer.

The best time to set the appointment time is before you actually receive the purchase agreement. You have a built-in reason for not discussing any aspects of the offer over the telephone. Try dialogue something like this:

Salesperson: "Mr. Seller, great news! Sarah Smith, a salesperson in my office, has written an agreement for the purchase of your house. I'm calling to see when we can meet to discuss it."
Seller: "Is it any good?"
Salesperson: "Sarah just called me and has not yet delivered the agreement to me. I can't give you any details, as I haven't seen the agreement yet. What I will do is update your seller's estimate sheet based on how the agreement was written after Sarah drops it off. Then we will be able to talk facts and figures when I stop by this evening."

Proceed to make an appointment.

If you already have received the agreement or written it yourself, use the following approach:

Salesperson: "Mr. Seller, this is Jim Londay. Great news! I've written a purchase agreement on your house. Could we meet this evening to discuss it?"
Seller: "Can you tell me what it is?"
Salesperson: "Mr. Seller, I could, but I prefer not to discuss something with as many aspects as a purchase agreement over the telephone. The possibility of a misunderstanding is just too great. Unless you have a strong objection, I prefer to wait until I meet with you face-to-face to discuss details."

If you have a strong constitution and have remained in control of your client, you should be able to politely decline questions when making the appointment. If working with a strong-willed, independent seller or if you find yourself consistently unable to avoid "spilling the beans," let someone else make the appointment for you. Your secretary, the receptionist in your office, or a fellow salesperson can handle the call for you. The following approach can be used if you are uncomfortable making the appointment yourself.

Receptionist: "Mr. Seller, good news! Jim Londay just called the office; he just has received a purchase agreement on your house. He is between appointments right now and asked me to call you to arrange a time to meet and discuss the agreement. He has two openings in his schedule, 4:00 this afternoon or 7:15 this evening. Would either of these times be good for you and your wife?"

When using this approach, it is best if your helper provides a choice of times from which the seller can choose.

Avoid discussing details of the agreement before meeting the sellers in person, whatever appointment-making approach you use. Giving sellers bits and pieces over the phone sets the stage for them to work themselves into a frenzied state over minor details before you can present the agreement in total.

PREPARATION

Before presenting the agreement, you first must assess the quality of the offer and decide how you will approach presenting it. If it is a good offer (one that, based on marketplace feedback, you feel the seller likely will not exceed), it is your moral and ethical duty as a fiduciary to get your sellers to accept the agreement as is, even they do not particularly like it. Your sellers hired you to act in their best interests. This sometimes means getting them to accept an agreement they are not enthused about initially.

Sellers do not always react to offers rationally. For this reason they need your guidance. They hired you to provide the best results possible. You frequently have to protect your sellers from their initial reaction to an offer. You cannot get more for a property than what it is worth as determined by the marketplace. Trying to squeeze an already good offer to get a little more is not worth the risk of losing the sale through possibly scaring off the buyer with a counteroffer.

Prospective purchasers of real estate are in a delicate state of mind. Buyers start rationalizing and convincing themselves they did the right thing the instant they hear their offer to purchase has been accepted. On the other hand, buyers have serious second thoughts whenever their original offer is countered. Many times, upon hearing their offer was not accepted, a buyer's first reaction is: "Perhaps we should look at a few more houses before we agree to pay this higher price." For these reasons it is wise to avoid writing a counteroffer unless an aspect of the offer absolutely requires a counteroffer for it to be acceptable. If the offer is close, get your sellers to accept it "as is."

GETTING OFFERS ACCEPTED "AS IS"

To get purchase offers accepted "as is" requires preparation on your part. It is the same as the preparation done prior to obtaining price adjustments (*see* Chapter 8, "Obtaining Price, Terms, and Condition Adjustments"). The following steps should be followed in preparing to present the offer to purchase:

1. Update Market Data   Compile all solds, pendings, expireds, and "on the markets" that have entered the system since you last updated the file.

2. Update Market Feedback   Update and collect all market feedback just as you do for obtaining adjustments. This includes: tour feedback, open house feedback, "Thanks for Showing My Listing" forms, and any other feedback you have received from prospective buyers who have seen the house or from salespersons who have seen or shown the house. Your sellers already will have seen much of this material but it is necessary to review it again to have the best chance to get the agreement accepted.

3. Update Mortgage Information and Research Selling Costs   Start by updating the mortgage and escrow balance of your sellers' current mortgage. If the owners have made any payments since the house was listed, the figures will have changed. In addition to obtaining the current principal balance and the amount in the escrow account, determine if there have been any disbursements made from the escrow account for property taxes or hazard insurance; a disbursement of this nature will change your proration figures.

Next, determine as closely as possible what your sellers' costs will be. Include any financing costs related to the purchaser's new loan that the seller will have to pay for under the terms of the agreement. The possibilities are: discount points to be paid by the sellers on some FHA and all VA loans, loan fees on many types of conventional loans, and any financing charges normally paid by the purchaser but included as a cost to the seller in the purchase agreement you are presenting.

Assembling these facts gives you a factual basis for recommending an "as is" acceptance when presenting a top-flight offer. Telling a seller, "This is the right thing to do," based on your feelings is not as effective as saying, "Based on this information, the marketplace has told us that we are not likely to do any better than this."

Using the updated mortgage and tax figures, prepare a new seller's estimate sheet based on how the agreement was written. This estimate sheet should be the only one you prepare if you feel the agreement is good and should be accepted "as is." Be armed to the teeth with ammunition supporting your recommendation for accepting the agreement as it was written whenever you feel that is the best course of action for your sellers to take.

PRESENTING THE OFFER

When you arrive for the presentation appointment, take a few minutes to set the stage. Get comfortable around the kitchen table and then get down to work. Be businesslike in your approach. After all, you are there to put together a sale. You are not on a social visit. Your sellers are anxious and want to get on with business.

Before distributing copies of the purchase agreement and seller's estimated net sheet, set the stage by saying:

> "Mr. and Mrs. Seller, I'd like to take a few minutes and briefly explain the ground rules of negotiating a real estate sale. Sellers involved in a real estate transaction have three ways in which they can respond to a written agreement. One is to accept the agreement as it was written with no alterations. After this acceptance is conveyed to the buyer, we have a binding agreement and can hold the purchaser's earnest money in our trust account as outlined in the agreement. A second option is to give a flat rejection of the offer as written. This effectively ends the negotiation unless the buyer chooses to write another offer. The remaining approach is to not accept or reject the agreement in its original form but to make a conditional acceptance of the agreement based on the buyer's agreeing to certain changes. In plain words, proposing a counteroffer."

Pause before saying the following:

> "We do not want to counter the agreement unless absolutely necessary because any counteroffer, no matter how small, voids the original agreement. Even if you are willing to accept the original agreement after a counteroffer is

turned down, you cannot do so unless the buyer decides to resubmit the original offer.

"Generally speaking, if an agreement is close to what a seller is looking for, it is best to accept it as it was written. In fact, it generally is agreed that it is advisable to counter an agreement only if there is some part of it that is significantly different from what a seller finds acceptable.

"You are interested in the bottom line. What we can net out of the sale is your primary consideration."

Note: Net proceeds are not always the primary consideration. In the rare cases when it is not, focus on the aspect of the sale most important to your seller.

"For that reason, I want you to look at the entire picture and not focus your total attention on one small, relatively insignificant point. I am sure you will agree with me that the most important figure we will discuss tonight is the amount of money you will net from the sale after all is said and done.

"The last point I want to make is the importance of looking at this agreement rationally and keeping emotions out of the negotiating progress. We don't want to antagonize and scare off a potential buyer by something said or implied in the heat of negotiation."

You may want to make this last point only if you have an agreement you are sure is going to be countered.

"The next thing I would like to do is update you on all market activity that has occurred since we last talked."

Distribute the updated final solds, pendings, expireds, and new listings at this point. Discuss each and how it relates to your sellers' situation.

Working Small to Big

Before distributing the actual offer to purchase, obtain conditional agreements on all relatively insignificant concessions the seller is being asked to make in the agreement. Save the major negotiation points until you have distributed the agreement. Small items are easier to sell when presented before major negotiating points are introduced.

Consider the following example. You have an offer for $3,000 less than the listing price. This falls in the range you consider fair and it is likely to be acceptable to your sellers. In addition to the reduced price, the buyer wants the sellers to leave a free-standing range/oven, an item excluded in the listing agreement. If possible, get a conditional agreement on leaving the range before discussing price:

> "Mr. and Mrs. Seller, the buyers have asked in the agreement they submitted that the range in the kitchen stay. If the rest of the agreement is acceptable, would you agree to leave the range?"

It is important to obtain this type of commitment. Including a used range a seller wanted to keep is not really a valid reason to turn down an otherwise acceptable offer. If the offer is acceptable otherwise, throw in the range and avoid the possibility of scaring the buyers off with a minor counteroffer.

Obtaining a conditional agreement on minor items like this before discussing price is relatively easy. Waiting until you have discussed price before mentioning the range, however, puts this minor part of the transaction in a different light. If you discuss price first, the seller's attitude often is:

> "I've already come down on the price, and they want the range, too!"

Obtaining the large concession first makes all subsequent small concessions seem bigger than they truly are. Resolve the small items first and save the heavy-duty negotiating for last.

After receiving conditional agreement on the minor points, distribute copies of the purchase agreement. Have a copy for every person present. Explain the entire agreement before having back-and-forth discussion on specific points:

> "Mr. and Mrs. Seller, I would like to explain the entire purchase agreement before we discuss any one portion of it. I have found that sellers best understand the buyer's position when using this approach."

Explaining the entire agreement before discussing specific points minimizes discussion on minor issues and lets you get right to the point on the significant aspects of the agreement. It focuses attention on the major points. Using presentation guidelines obtained from your manager, work patiently with your sellers until they completely understand how the agreement was written. The agreement may not be acceptable to your sellers but it is necessary for them to have a complete grasp of it in order to decide what to do.

Obtaining the Acceptance

Make a serious effort to get the agreement accepted without change if in your opinion the offer is fair, has been written clearly, and it is in your sellers' best interests to accept it. Explaining the seller's net sheet provides an excellent closing opportunity when presenting what you believe to be an acceptable agreement. Present the estimated net sheet, explaining each expense in detail. Make sure your sellers have a complete understanding of the net sheet and the purchase agreement before you close for the signature. Sellers are more likely to accept an agreement if they have a full understanding of it.

After the agreement and seller's net sheet have been explained, merely turn the net sheet toward your sellers, circle the estimated net, and say something like this:

> "Mr. and Mrs. Seller, this will be your approximate net if you accept this agreement."

Do not talk. In this, as in many negotiating situations, the first person to speak makes the concession. There may be an uncomfortable silence for what seems to be a long time but, as noted earlier, it is more uncomfortable for the sellers than it is for you. If there is a possibility that they will accept the agreement without countering, it will become apparent at this point.

Often a significant amount of time will elapse with no one speaking. This is a strong indicator that your sellers are ready to sign if given a small nudge. This setting calls for the use of the "silent assumptive close." Without speaking, assemble the agreements with carbons, fill in the acceptance blanks, mark X's indicating where the signatures go, and place the assembled agreements directly between the sellers. Do this without saying a word and wait. Wait until something happens. Often one of the sellers silently will take the agreements and sign them.

If the assumptive close fails, it is usually because your sellers have unresolved questions or concerns. Working at a pace they are comfortable with, review the agreement in detail. Keep inquiring until you determine their specific objections or concerns. A good way to do this is to have the sellers do what Ben Franklin did when making a big decision: List the pros and cons and weigh the benefits. After you have pinpointed the sticking points, refer back to the materials you assembled and again make your case that, based on the available *facts*, the offer is good and should be accepted. When facing a large decision, people see problems and concerns as being larger than they really are. Be persuasive in putting things in perspective and be persistent in attempting to get the signatures.

PREPARING A COUNTEROFFER

If the agreement will have to be countered, use your preparation and research to obtain the best counter possible. Some general principles follow.

Take the Big Leap

Counter at the lowest price and the best terms for the buyer that the seller will take. Avoid going back and forth. For example: You have a property listed at $88,000 and receive an offer of $80,000. Your seller wants to go back at full price or maybe $87,000. In most cases this will at best ensure receiving another counteroffer at around $81,000. If you get started on $1,000 concessions, the negotiations are doomed. You will be involved in a back-and-forth situation and before you know it the buyer or seller, or both, will be angry. The buyer will walk and you will have lost the sale. **In working with buyers and sellers, the size of the concessions made in many cases is not as problematic as the number of *times* concessions are made.**
Approach taking the big leap this way:

> "Mr. Seller, I understand your wanting to counter at $87,000 but before you do, let me ask you a question. If it came down to it, would you accept an offer of $84,000?"

Press hard to find the seller's true position. If the answer is "yes" and the marketplace tells you that it is as well as you are likely to do, tell him he should counter at $84,000. Let the seller know that you will inform the selling salesperson that $84,000 is the bottom figure and that the counteroffer was made in a good-faith effort to avoid petty back-and-forth negotiation. Repetitive back-and-forth negotiating destroys sales, and this fact can and in most cases should be explained to your buyer. Taking the big leap works more often than not in getting an agreement cemented. The odds are put in the sellers' favor because the negotiations are brought to a critical stage at the soonest possible time.

Counter Only One Item

When countering an offer is necessary, limit the number of items included in the counter. If possible, counter only one item. Going back with a laundry list of counters in most cases ensures a turndown or yet another counter with an equally large number of items in dispute. Use an approach similar to:

> "Mrs. Seller, I understand your desire to counter this list of relatively small items. But the best negotiation strategy is to counter only one item if possible. Let me explain why.
> "Every item you counter sets the stage for a battle that the selling salesperson has to win with the buyer. I would rather see you counter at a higher price and drop this list than include them all and counter at a lower price. In that way the selling salesperson can approach the buyer in the following way: 'Mr. and Mrs. Buyer, great news! Your offer has been accepted with only one exception.'"

The one exception might be $6,000 but it is still only *one* objection that needs to be overcome.

> "For these reasons, Mrs. Seller, I recommend you leave the mirrors, the refrigerator, the bar, and the window coverings, and counter only the price, based on what you will accept as a net figure."

Bite the Bullet on the Small Stuff

You must discourage your sellers from making minor counteroffers. If they want to counter a $200 item, tell them of the risk involved:

> "Mr. Seller, you hired me to get the most we can out of your property. By countering a relatively small item, we are

not working toward that purpose. Any counter, no matter how small, all too often results in the buyers catching a case of 'Buyer's Remorse' after which they back out of the sale. This is a good offer. It's time to bite the bullet on the small stuff, accept this offer, and have the peace of mind that comes with knowing your house is sold."

Weigh the Risks

When trying to eliminate or minimize counters, stress the costs involved for the sellers if the buyer decides to walk away. If the sellers lose a buyer over a matter of $500 and do not see another buyer for three months, they have not only lost the sale but probably cost themselves thousands of dollars in additional payments, utility bills, insurance, and upkeep. In addition they still have the hassle of not having sold their property.

Handle Upset Sellers

On occasion sellers are upset over the set of circumstances they are in. Many times this occurs during a forced sale caused by the sellers' financial difficulties. Have empathy for their situation. These sellers are frustrated and their anger is understandable. Unfortunately, you often will be the focal point for their frustration after you bring them an offer. The amount offered, although a fair price, may not be enough to solve their financial problems. Understand that what they say is not personally directed toward you. It may sound that way but it is not.

No matter how upset your sellers become, and no matter what names they call you or things they say about you, you cannot afford to lose your cool. If you do, you also lose the sale. Be their relief valve and let them get rid of the pressure. Do not get upset. After they have the frustration out of their systems, you will be able to talk business, make the most of the situation you have to work with, and take the steps that are best for them.

Provide Alternate Seller's Estimate Sheets

When presenting a contract you are sure will be countered, prepare seller's estimated net sheets based on the price you feel the counteroffer should be. Without having written suggestions in this form, you will be forced to use the seller's initial reaction as a starting point. All too often, a seller's reaction to an unrealistically low offer is, "To heck with 'em, tell 'em to give me my price or forget it!" By being prepared with written suggestions in the form of prepared seller's estimate sheets, you increase the chances of obtaining a reasonable counter.

Use the "Reversal Technique"

When your sellers are reluctant to accept a good offer or make a reasonable counteroffer, ask:

> "Please try to be objective and answer this question as if you were the prospective buyer. After seeing the market data we've reviewed, would you pay as much for this house as you are asking these buyers to pay?"

If they say "yes," review the market data and ask them to show you a basis for their position.

HELPING THE SALESPERSON GET THE COUNTEROFFER ACCEPTED

First, provide the salesperson with the same market data you have prepared for and given the sellers. This provides the salesperson with facts he or she can use to support the counteroffered price when attempting to get the counter accepted. It demonstrates the need and basis for making the counter. The fact that the seller has valid reasons based on market data for altering the agreement as it was originally written makes it easier for the buyer to accept it.

Second, include two clauses in your counteroffer (*see* Example 25).

The first is: "The seller reserves the right to negotiate and accept other agreements for the sale of this property until written acceptance of this counteroffer is delivered to the seller's salesperson." This is a right the sellers already have. They can negotiate with as many different buyers at the same time as they like. This phrase is included in the counteroffer to create urgency with the prospective buyer. Many prospective buyers think that because they are negotiating in writing with the seller that they have an exclusive option on the property. This inclusion is a way of letting the buying prospects know they are risking losing the property to another purchaser if they do not act in a timely manner.

Example 25

LONDAY
Real Estate Company

SAMPLE OF AN UNDERSTANDABLE, READABLE COUNTEROFFER

The seller accepts the foregoing offer with the following exceptions:

1. Price to be $87,500.

2. Seller to pay no more than three (3) discount points on the buyer's new loan; loan not to exceed $65,000.

3. The seller reserves the right to negotiate and accept other agreements for the sale of this property until written acceptance of this counteroffer is delivered to the seller's salesperson.

4. This counteroffer is to be considered withdrawn and void if not accepted by 10:00 P.M., February 6, 19__.

Note: The written parts of offers or counteroffers are always more easily understoon if each item is numbered. Clause 3 does not give the sellers any rights they do not already have under the contract law. This and Clause 4 are included to inject urgency into the negotiations. Clauses 3 and 4 should be a part of every counteroffer.

Suite 402, Hillcrest Landing, Omaha, NE 68127
(402) 733-5443

The second inclusion is: "This counteroffer is void if not accepted by _____." Use common sense when setting this deadline. This is added to avoid the "Let's wait a week and make the same offer" thinking on the part of the buyers. They still have the option to wait but a deadline gives the selling salesperson some leverage to use in keeping the negotiations going. Once negotiations cool off, they are very hard to put into motion again.

If you have a seller who wants to sell and a buyer who wants to buy, a professional salesperson can figure out a way to make it work. Putting together sales where the buyer and seller start out miles apart is the mark of a true professional in the real estate business. Write and rewrite agreements until you have a meeting of the minds.

CHAPTER 10

STRUCTURING A SMOOTH CLOSING

Closing a real estate sale can be exhilarating, trying, satisfying, and sometimes even comical—all at the same time. Dozens of people are involved between the time the purchase agreement is written and the sale is closed. Appraisers, loan officers, termite inspectors, loan processors, underwriters, title insurance company reps—you could add to the list indefinitely. Each has a job to do and if only one of them does not do it, you will not close on time.

MONITORING PROGRESS

One of the unwritten duties you have to a seller is to orchestrate the events and motivate the many people involved. You have the ultimate responsibility of making sure everyone else will be ready. Monitor the progress of your pending sales continuously. An easy way to do this is to make notations in your appointment book of the dates on which every step of the closing process should be completed. Include reminders on the dates by which credit check, appraisal, loan approval, termite inspection, title binder, and so forth should be received.

Do not assume that things will be ready when they should be. Regularly review each pending file. If a lawyer tells you he will have a child support lien released and recorded by the fifth, call him on the sixth to make sure it was done. If appraisals normally take ten working days in your locale, make a note in your appointment book to call the loan officer two weeks after the sale was written to see if the appraisal has come in. If the appraisal has come in, you probably will know about it and will not need to make the call. But if it has not come in, your appointment book will remind you to check and speed things along. By following up faithfully, you will catch mistakes early and increase your chances of avoiding unnecessary delays. Some salespersons set aside one afternoon or morning each week to follow up on each of their pending sales. It does not matter how you do it, but follow up every pending sale in a consistent way.

In addition to working with the seller, the four main groups of people you will work with are loan officers and processors; appraisers and underwriters for the FHA, VA, and private mortgage insurance firms; the selling agent; and attorneys. Finding the right people to work with—when you have a choice—and helping them do their jobs will ensure the smoothest possible closing. After examining the continuing relationship with the seller, we will look at each of these four groups.

WORKING WITH THE SELLERS

Get off to a good start by preparing the sellers for the sometimes crazy and unexpected twists you may encounter in your quest to deliver their proceeds check. Immediately after agreement with the buyer is reached, meet with your sellers to outline and explain the normal sequence of events during the pending period.

Prepare them for the visits from the appraiser, termite inspector, surveyor, and anyone else who will need to make an on-site inspection of the property. These could include: inspections by home warranty company personnel, city code inspectors, furnacemen, and those conducting any other type of inspection specified in the agreement. Discover what tasks you will need to complete before closing by arranging for these inspections immediately after the agreement is reached. The sellers will then have adequate time to complete any required repairs and resolve any easement rights conflicts. Prepare the sellers for what they will encounter during the pending period by outlining the sequence of events that will occur before closing.

WORKING WITH BANKERS

Good loan officers put money in the bank for your seller and for you. They get loans approved faster and sales closed more quickly than the average loan officer. Whenever possible, place loans with a top-notch loan officer you have worked with in the past. You will be assured that the buyer's loan will be approved if at all possible and the sale will be closed in a timely fashion.

After the loan application has taken place, you can put a number of practices into effect to aid the loan officer in obtaining swift approval of the application. First, before the loan application appointment takes place, inform the loan officer about any potential stumbling blocks in obtaining approval of which you are aware. Getting potential problems out on the table gives the loan officer the best opportunity of getting the loan approved at the earliest date. You can help the loan officer in a number of other ways. Tell the buyers what they will need to bring to the loan appointment. Supply them with a written checklist outlining all the information, documentation, and checks that they will need to give the loan officer. Bring or provide copies of the listing agreement, sales agreement, personal property agreements, etc. These are necessary to get the loan processing started in a timely manner.

A salesperson's working relationship with a loan officer is at its most critical when there is difficulty in getting a loan approved. When loan approval is at an apparent dead end, look at the transaction from the loan officer's perspective. Loan officers have to sell loans to the underwriter, whether it is their own loan committee, a private mortgage insurer, the VA, the FHA, or another government agency. Look at the sale from different points of view and try to repackage it in a form that the underwriter reviewing the loan will approve.

Possibilities include gift letters, consolidation loans to improve ratios, and letters or affidavits explaining valid reasons for poor marks on the credit report. A workable solution that the loan officer has not considered is often possible. Salespersons and buyers assume loan officers explore every financing avenue on every loan they process. This is not necessarily true. By being closer to the sale, you may be in a better position to consider and explore alternate possibilities for obtaining approval. Develop enough tenacity and determination to repackage and resubmit loans for approval time and time again until every conceivable possibility is exhausted.

WORKING WITH PUBLIC SERVANTS

This group of people includes, but is not limited to, building inspectors, underwriters, reviewers, architects, and supervisory personnel. They may be employed by various federal government agencies: the FHA, the VA, Ginnie Mae, Fannie Mae, etc. Other possibilities are state and local government civil servants whose specific authorities will have a bearing on your sale. They may include building inspectors on new home sales and city code inspectors on sales involving certain types of government-insured or guaranteed refinancing.

Understanding how the system works will aid you in getting results. The nature of a public servant's job requires a justification in writing for every action taken and every decision made. The loan approvals they grant have to fit into or fall under the thousands of rules and regulations by which they live and die. The basis for every exception they make to the rules has to be in a form that can be included in their files. After you understand this basic fact of bureaucratic life, you will be able to obtain approvals that otherwise would never make it.

Affidavits frequently can be used to obtain an exception. They can be tailored to solve almost any problem you encounter. Affidavits do not change the problem; they merely provide a justification for approving a loan, granting waivers, or making specific exceptions that will allow you to scale the mountains of red tape and achieve the approvals you need.

The following is an example of obtaining governmental cooperation. I worked with a young couple interested in buying one of my listings, but the only program under which they qualified was a state-sponsored mortgage fund. We had a problem: Although they were the type of people the program was designed to help, they did not meet one of the technical requirements. I approached a number of loan officers, all of whom saw no way to make the sale work. I was determined that these young people would not be denied the opportunity to buy their first house because of a technicality.

I contacted the head of the agency administering the program and explained the situation to him, including the fact that a technicality was the only roadblock keeping this couple from purchasing the house. We discussed the details of the proposed transaction, after which I told him that I had approached him personally because I wanted to find a way to qualify the buyers while complying with the spirit and letter of the rules. I was not getting any cooperation elsewhere. I further explained that I felt the situation was such that the loan could and should be approved. After a series of phone calls, a solution of producing a signed affidavit explaining the basis for an exception was worked out. The loan was approved, the young couple bought their first house, I got paid, and the system was satisfied.

WORKING WITH ATTORNEYS

The extent to which attorneys become involved in real estate closings varies widely in different parts of the country. In some areas attorneys rarely attend or have anything to do with real estate closings. In other locales attorneys routinely are involved in virtually every real estate transaction. Whatever the extent of the involvement by attorneys in your part of the country, the principles you apply in working with them are the same.

Inform the attorney of progress prior to his or her involvement in the sale. Reach an understanding on what needs to be done (and when) in order to close the sale as planned. Optimum results are achieved by giving the attorney as much time as you can to do the job, plus verifying in writing what all parties in the transaction are to complete to ensure a trouble-free closing. Speed the process by promptly supplying the attorney with what he or she needs to handle his or her part of the transaction (title binder, purchase agreement, amortization schedule, survey, etc.).

Personally meeting with an attorney when working with a particularly complex sale can aid in avoiding misunderstandings. At this meeting you can learn how every portion of the transaction is to be processed. This gives you an opportunity to confirm what was agreed on to that point, how it was arrived at, and why it was done that way. You pave the way to a smooth closing by reaching a thorough understanding in advance of what is to occur.

WORKING WITH THE BUYER'S SALESPERSON

There are several ways in which a listing agent can work with the buyer's salesperson in effecting a timely closing. Start by keeping track of the details in the nuts-and-bolts part of the transaction. Be prompt in returning purchase agreements, depositing earnest money, ordering appraisals, and returning phone calls. Extra attention is called for when the selling salesperson is relatively inexperienced. At times these salespersons feel somewhat lost and will accept and appreciate any understanding and support you can give them. Work closely with any relatively new salespersons to make sure they are obtaining all the assistance they need to confidently handle their end of the closing. Treat them as equals and make yourself available if they seek your help.

WORKING WITH APPRAISERS

You can do a number of things to ensure receiving the best possible appraisal. First, get the seller to have the house looking its absolute best when the appraiser comes to do his or her inspection. Second, give the appraiser some unsolicited assistance. Assemble the comparable solds that best justify the sales price of the sold property and make sure the appraiser receives them. An easy way to do this is to place them in an envelope and tape them to the door right next to the lockbox or on the refrigerator door of the property. Label the envelope: "For Real Estate Appraiser." Providing the appraiser with these data makes sure that the appraiser has the best available market data with which to work. This is another of the small things you can do to ensure that your seller receives every dollar possible out of the sale.

View yourself as the glue that holds sales together. Accept the responsibility of acting as an unofficial coordinator of events while making sure you do not interfere in another sphere of responsibility. (The specific responsibilities of each salesperson in closing the sale differ depending on region.) Taking care of the details and following up to make sure things get done on time assure the most trouble-free closings possible.

PART V

BUILDING REFERRALS AND REPEAT BUSINESS

CHAPTER 11

THE FUTURE FILE

"I want someone who needs to do business today!" We all do. That is the reason we prospect. Buyers and sellers with immediate needs are always a professional's first priority. Prospecting is the basis upon which all success in residential real estate sales is built. In almost all prospecting a salesperson is looking for a customer with immediate needs. But in addition to being a source of immediate listings, prospecting provides us with homeowners thinking of selling but not yet ready to place their houses on the market. These prospects form the basis of your Future File.

HOW DO I FIND THEM?

Direct-Mail Prospecting

Homeowners expecting to sell their houses in six to eighteen months often respond to a well-planned direct-mail campaign (*see* Chapter 3, "Direct-Mail Prospecting"). They often request that a market analysis be prepared on their property even though they had not planned to call a salesperson at the time they received the direct-mail solicitation. Direct-mail prospecting frequently provides you with the opportunity to be first in line with a large number of sellers who plan to put their houses on the market in the near future.

Working Expireds

When working expireds, you will find that a certain number of listings that appear to be expireds are actually cancelled listings. These are a bountiful source of prospects for your Future File. In many instances homeowners who have cancelled their listings have done so because their proposed moves were postponed. In many cases circumstances change again and these people become immediate prospects within six months to a year. You also will find that many owners of expired listings have exhausted their patience and energy in trying to sell their property. Unless a move is mandated by outside circumstances, many of these owners take their house off the market vowing to "keep it forever!" In most cases the original reasons for their wanting to sell have not changed. In most of these instances the property is back on the market within six months.

Phone- or Door-Canvassing

Many find cold-call phone-canvassing or door-knocking to be effective and enjoyable ways to locate business. This type of prospecting naturally uncovers more Future File prospects than homeowners who are ready to list and sell their property immediately.

Personal Referrals/Permanent Customer File

People who make up your personal customer file provide numerous Future File leads. Frequent contact with people in your permanent file using newsletters and other follow-up techniques maximizes the number of Future File leads received from this source (*see* Chapter 12, "Developing a Loyal Clientele").

Other Sources

Highly successful real estate people view every business, personal, or incidental social contact as a potential source of leads. Many develop Future File leads and eventual listings from manning open houses, receiving calls from sign riders, during a visit to the dentist, and stopping at the store for a loaf of bread. Whenever the subject of real estate comes up, and do not hesitate to initiate the conversation yourself, be awake and receptive to any mention of people considering a sale of their house.

ESTABLISH INDIVIDUAL PROSPECT FILES

You should take a number of steps upon discovering a Future File prospect. The first is to prepare a market analysis for the prospect. I realize that the prospect is not ready to sell. In fact in many cases the property owner is not looking for a market analysis at the time you approach him or her. Forge ahead. Your purpose in doing a market analysis at this point is not to list the house but to establish yourself and shut out the competition.

The initial dialogue usually goes somewhat like this:

> Salesperson: "Mr. Prospect, this is Jim Londay, with Londay Real Estate Company. I was chatting with a mutual friend of ours, Ron Cappola, and he mentioned that you were considering selling your house."
> Prospect: "That's right, but I don't plan on putting my house on the market until spring, possibly even summer."

At this point discuss the sellers' plans, where they are going, and what their motivations are. If they are considering a move out of town, explore the possibility of referring them to a salesperson in that city. When this phase of the discussion comes to a natural conclusion, proceed in the following vein:

> Salesperson: "Mr. Prospect, with your permission, I would like to prepare a market analysis of your property at this time. I realize you are not even sure you are moving but I think you would find it helpful to have an idea what you would net from a sale when you do decide if you are going to move or not. Of course there is no cost or obligation in my preparing an analysis of your property."

Make an appointment. If you do not get in the door with this approach, your phone technique or your choice of approach or dialogue needs improvement. When approaching a Future File prospect, it is reasonable to expect to get an appointment in virtually every case. After all, you are providing a valuable service at no cost or obligation to the prospect. Getting the appointment before another salesperson gets in the door is important. If you are not consistently successful, analyze your approach and vary it to find an approach and wording that work for you.

Once the appointment is made, approach and treat the prospects as if they were thinking of listing their property immediately. Conduct the measure-up appointment as if they were ready to list on that day. Prepare a complete market analysis. You will have to do the work eventually. By doing it before your prospect expects it, you create a favorable impression. When presenting your market analysis, proceed exactly as you would for an immediate prospect but leave out the trial and final closes. You will create an exceptionally favorable impression with the prospect. The fact that you have prepared an in-depth market analysis, taken the time to explain it, and answered their questions gives you an almost insurmountable edge over any salesperson who subsequently comes along and tries to obtain the listing. I have had prospects in this situation who were so grateful that they sent *me* thank-you notes. If you follow up correctly, this approach provides you with a virtual lock on the listing when the prospect gets ready to sell.

Immediately following the presentation of your market analysis, send a handwritten thank-you note to your new prospects. Add them to your permanent customer file and your Future File. When your prospect is ready to market the property, simply update the market data portion and prepare a new seller's estimate sheet. Also prepare a marketing schedule (*see* Chapter 6, "Preparing the Listing Presentation") at the time the property is placed on the market.

Keep a separate file folder for every person in your Future File. Individual files should contain the initial market analysis, subsequent updates, source of the prospect, copies of thank-you notes and correspondence, and short, written summaries of every telephone or in-person contact you have with the prospect. Most salespersons find it impossible to remember every conversation they have with their prospects and customers. However, your customers are likely to remember in detail every conversation they have with you. They remember the specifics you talked about because their potential sale is the only real estate transaction they are keeping track of. By keeping good notes for reference, you will be able to recall the details of each prospect's situation whenever he or she calls you.

Keep your Future File close to the telephone you most

frequently use for business. When a Future File prospect calls, you will be able to pull the file and immediately start discussing specifics. I also suggest keeping a duplicate Future File prospect list in a safe place separate from your regular records. In this way, if a disaster—a fire, for example—obliterates your records, you will not have to recreate your entire Future File from memory, which is an impossible task.

Set up your Future File in a way that is comfortable for you. The format is not as important as keeping it simple. Keep comprehensive records for every prospect in your file. Organize the file in such a way that follow-up and reference to specific files can be done easily and quickly.

SERVICING THE FUTURE FILE

Future File prospects will be on your newsletter mailing list and receive the same benefits (calendars, Christmas cards) as does every customer on your permanent list (*see* Chapter 12, "Developing a Loyal Clientele"). In addition, Future File prospects are placed on an intensified schedule of telephone contacts and personal visits. The frequency will vary with how close the prospects are to placing their houses on the market. If they are indefinite in their plans and do not realistically expect to move for a year, monthly contact is sufficient. If their prospects for moving are more immediate—if they are waiting for transfer orders, for example—weekly or even daily contact may be called for. Base your frequency of contact on how soon they think they will move and how they respond to your calls and visits. It is unwise to let a Future File contact go longer than one month without a phone or mail contact from you.

Future File prospects also should be contacted whenever there is a change in the local market that has an effect on the salability of their property. Changes in interest rates, the initiation of new loan programs, the development by your company of new promotional or advertising programs, etc., should prompt a visit or telephone call from you. Work hard to be your prospects' source of information on current activities in your local real estate market. This builds the type of loyalty that assures you the listing when the house is placed on the market.

Updating Market Activity

Initiate a program in which you update the market activity in the immediate area for each prospect in your Future File every three or six months. Include all sales, pendings, expireds, and new listings for each owner of a property in your Future File every time you prepare an update. Mail or deliver the information to each prospect.

This sounds like a lot of work but is not. If your MLS is computerized, it will take only minutes to run updated market data for each of your Future File prospects and drop the information in the mail. You will be filling otherwise nonproductive time at the office in a way that pays off in customer loyalty and referrals.

Mail Contacts

An excellent way to humanize prospect follow-up is to send them newspaper or magazine clippings relating to their jobs or personal interests. Do this whenever you come across an article in which one of your Future File prospects would have an interest. The article you clip and mail does not have to relate to business or real estate. Articles relating to your prospect's hobbies or interests are also effective. Clipping an article and dropping it in the mail takes just a minute and lets prospects know you took a personal interest in them, remember them, and are thinking of them. Clip the article, write a short note on it, and drop it in an envelope addressed to the prospect along with one of your business cards.

Subscribe to the *Wall Street Journal* and one or more business periodicals such as *Forbes* or *Business Week*. In addition to providing a source of clippings, these newspapers and periodicals will enable you to discuss many of the topics brought up by your prospects in a knowledgeable way. The more informed you are, the more likely your prospects will be to accept and follow your advice when pricing and marketing their real estate.

BENEFITS OF THE FUTURE FILE

This program, properly administered, provides a phenomenal success ratio. You will list a large majority of the properties in your Future File that are eventually placed on the market. These prospects are one of the most neglected groups of selling prospects in residential real estate sales. A salesperson who capitalizes on this fact will make a lot of money. Organizing your system and devoting a mere two hours a week to following up on your Future File will produce unparalleled results for the time and effort expended. Your success ratio should easily exceed 50 percent and in some cases 75 percent of your Future File prospects that eventually go on the market.

An added benefit is the referral business you will receive from the people in your file. Because of the unusual amount of attention properly serviced Future File prospects receive, you will be the first person thought of when the subject of real estate comes up.

By organizing a Future File, a salesperson can provide himself or herself with the first and greatest opportunity of listing a potentially large number of properties. Candidates for a Future File prospect list come from a wide variety of sources. Alert salespersons will track down and work every prospect they hear of.

If organized correctly, one salesperson can effectively service 50 to 75 Future File prospects in two to three hours a week. A Future File with 50 valid prospects should yield an average of one to two listings per month. By making your Future File a separate, self-contained entity, you can avoid the common problem of neglecting or forgetting about potential sellers who are preparing to place their houses on the market in the near future.

CHAPTER 12

DEVELOPING A LOYAL CLIENTELE

Building and nurturing a loyal clientele provides a professional with phenomenal benefits over the long term. Salespersons should devote a percentage of their time to building, updating, and servicing a permanent customer file immediately upon entering the business. Waiting to build and maintain a solid customer base postpones the receipt of profitable referral business. The people that make up your permanent customer file will be your principal source of leads.

THE NATURE OF REFERRALS

Individuals will refer business to a salesperson only when they see that person as a knowledgeable professional interested in helping them or their friends solve real estate problems.

Knowing the local marketplace and being willing to work hard are not enough. To obtain referrals, your name has to be the first thing that comes to a person's mind when the subject of real estate comes up. The old saw "It's who you know that counts" does not count when it comes to referrals. Who knows YOU is what counts.

Getting people to send you referral business takes planning and persistence. The more contacts you have with a person, the more likely that person will be to think of you whenever talk turns to real estate. The more frequently you contact a customer, the more likely he or she will be to remember you when a referral opportunity occurs. Every contact with past and prospective customers is helpful. Telephone calls, personal visits, seeing people at the grocery store—they all count. You will find as your customer list grows that it becomes more difficult and ultimately impossible to personally contact all the people on your list often enough to maintain them as loyal customers. There are not enough hours in the day to keep in personal contact with 600 people and leave time for listing and selling houses, not to mention your personal life.

The only practical solution is to let the mail carrier work for you by sending each of your customers a newsletter promoting you and your company. Aggressive application of a newsletter program does not mean you can forget about keeping in touch with phone calls and personal visits. Personal contacts always will be the most effective recognition-builder in a salesperson's portfolio of techniques and should be employed as often as practical. The individual practices you can use to build loyalty, expand your referral business, and ultimately increase your income are:

- Servicing Your Present Customers
- Working with Referrals
- Responding to a Botched Referral
- Referring Referrals
- Developing a Newsletter Program
- Mailing Personal Notes and Thank-Yous
- Prospecting Tombstone Files
- Personal Prospecting

SERVICING YOUR PRESENT CUSTOMERS AND REFERRALS

Every request for service, large or small, from a customer should receive prompt and thorough attention. When handling requests, little things make a big difference. Consider the following example: A customer calls and asks if origination fees can be deducted on his or her federal income tax form, and you are not sure of the answer. The easy way is to refer him or her to the IRS or an accountant. If he or she was comfortable doing that, you would never have received a call.

Handle this request by saying "I am not sure. I will find out for you and call you back." Find the answer. Get the regulation title and number and call your customer. Answer the question and ask if he or she wants a copy of the regulation. By approaching the request in this way, you will reinforce the very attitude that prompted this person to call you in the first place. Treat every request for help as if your professional livelihood depended on it, because it does.

You likewise owe prospects referred to you the best service you are capable of delivering. These potential buyers and sellers were referred to you because the person originating the referral believed enough in your abilities to recommend you to a friend or acquaintance. You need to live up to the trust these people put in you.

You lose in two ways when you fail to provide superior service to referral prospects. First, you risk losing an immediate sale or listing. This is a lost commission you will never get back. Second, and far more important, you risk alienating the customer who referred the prospect to you. Whenever a salesperson does a poor job with a referral, the person originating the referral feels foolish. News of poor service always gets back to the person making the referral. You can be sure that he or she will never send you referrals in the future.

You have an obligation to every person who refers potential customers to you to do what is expected: Handle referred business promptly and thoroughly. At times this includes handling business you would rather not have. Consider this example: You normally work in the $100,000 to $125,000 price range. You get a telephone call from a person to whom you have previously sold a house. The conversation goes like this:

Customer: "Marilyn! Dave Smithberg here. How have you been?"

Salesperson: "Just fine! How about you?"

C: "Fine, thanks. The reason I'm calling is that my favorite niece finally married her sweetheart a few months ago. She and her husband are looking for a house. When I heard about it, I naturally thought of you. I've never forgotten the fine job you did when you sold Mary and me our present home."

S: "Tell me about your niece and her husband."

C: "Oh, they are really excited about buying a house. But they only can afford something for around $30,000."

In this salesperson's market $30,000 barely will buy something to keep the elements out, but to the couple buying their first house it is the fulfillment of a dream. The commission on a sale of this size may not be worth the time and effort involved to an established salesperson, but any salesperson worth his or her salt will spend the time needed to place these buyers in the best $30,000 house possible.

Superior salespersons give superior service. The amount of the commission makes no difference. You obtain referral business in only one way: by earning it. Earn it by satisfying your customers' needs. Place their needs above all else. By putting your customers' concerns first, you do not have to worry about commissions. A handsome commission income will be the automatic result.

Responding to a Botched Referral

On occasion you may find yourself in the position of having failed with a referred client. If this happens, work quickly to minimize the damage, whatever the reason for the failure. Start by contacting the person who referred the prospect to you. Try an opening similar to:

> "Charlie, I'm calling to let you know that your neighbor's son and daughter-in-law found the perfect house for themselves. Unfortunately, I didn't find it for them. I'm not concerned with that, the most important thing is that they found the right house at the right price. I'm sorry I couldn't be the one who found it for them, especially since you referred them to me. Still, I wanted to call to let you know how things ended up and to thank you for sending the referral to me in the first place."

Next, contact the young couple and congratulate them on the fine buy they made. Also include the buyers on your newsletter mailing list. In two years they will probably think you sold them the house in the first place! Make the best of a bad situation by being conscientious in following up to minimize possible damage to your relationship with your referral source.

Referring Referrals

On occasion you will receive a referral you would be unwise to accept. An example is a request for an appraisal that you are not qualified to prepare or a referral of a buyer who is looking for property outside of your area of knowledge. The latter could be a prospective buyer for commercial or industrial property, an area in which you may have no experience and do not feel qualified to help.

At times you may encounter the pleasant problem of being so busy that you cannot take on the referral because of time commitments already made to other customers. Or perhaps you are leaving town the next day for a two-week vacation. Whatever the reason, whenever you should not or cannot work a referral, arrange for the prospect to work with a salesperson you know is capable of providing great service. If you can arrange to receive a referral fee, fine. But do not let this be the guiding factor. Keep the prospect's interests first.

DEVELOPING A NEWSLETTER PROGRAM

Few salespersons understand how important a regularly mailed newsletter is to building their referral business. An aggressive newsletter program is the backbone of any customer servicing program. New salespersons often put off initiating a newsletter program because they feel they do not have enough people to mail to and because of the cost. This is a costly mistake. Small savings incurred when new in the business translate into reduced income in future months and years. Instituting a quality newsletter program immediately upon entering the real estate business is one of the most intelligent moves a new licensee can make. After salespersons realize the profit potential, they maintain, promote, and expand the newsletter throughout their careers.

For best results mail newsletters to every person in your permanent customer file a minimum of six times a year. Fewer than six issues a year greatly reduces the program's impact. You can produce your own newsletter or subscribe to a newsletter service. Subscribing to a service is preferable. Purchasing newsletters from a newsletter publisher has many advantages. The majority of these publishers individualize the newsletters with the salesperson's name, photo, and company logo on the front page. They put out a more professional-looking product than a salesperson who writes and puts together his or her own letter can produce. The format is consistent issue to issue, making it quickly recognizable to your customers.

Another advantage is a significant time savings. A salesperson's time is too valuable to be spent sitting in an office writing, assembling, and producing a newsletter. Remember, you should be spending the majority of your time working with prospects. The last major advantage in using a newsletter service is that newsletter publishers print issues on a regular basis. By ordering every issue you ensure frequent and regular contact with the people that make up your permanent customer file.

The only potential disadvantage of using a service is that you have limited control over the content. In most cases these newsletters are well written and interesting and the fact that you do not control the content usually is not a problem. Because they have to be written for all parts of the country, however, the information is general in nature. Specifics about your local market cannot be incorporated.

The only real advantage of writing and publishing your own newsletter is the opportunity to tailor it to your locale. This advantage is usually not enough to offset the disadvantages. If you do have significant news you would like to share, write a supplement and include it with your publisher-purchased newsletters. Material in these supplements can include information about new loan programs, changes in local market conditions, interest rate news, and other news of local interest. A popular insert is a list of local service people, what they do, and how to contact them. Babysitters, painters, plumbers, handypeople, teenagers willing to mow lawns, and car-starting services are good inclusions. Also popular are suggestions for good restaurants, nightclubs, museums, and plays. Anecdotes and comments about personal experiences while attending these places and events add interest.

The biggest obstacle in writing your own newsletter is the plain fact that salesperson-produced newsletters do not get written and mailed on a regular basis. I know of no salesperson who puts out his or her own newsletter as often as planned. The most conscientious salesperson I know who writes his own newsletter tries to publish nine issues a year. He enjoys advantages many salespersons do not have. He owns a word processor and has his own personal secretary. Although he works hard and is well organized, he is lucky to get out six issues a year. The majority of salespersons writing their own newsletters do not do as well and give up self-written newsletters after two or three issues. They find that buying newsletters from a service is more cost-effective, time-effective, and consistent.

Consistency is what makes a newsletter program successful. You will notice a significant increase in referral business in the two weeks following the mailing of your newsletters. In addition to increased referrals and customer loyalty, my customers thank me for keeping in touch with them.

One last tip about newsletters: Always include a photo of yourself on your newsletters and on every other type of advertising or mailer you use. I was convinced of the importance of this when I first met the wife of a longtime friend of mine. She said she felt like she had known me for years because she had seen the photo on my newsletter so often.

PERSONAL NOTES AND THANK-YOU'S

Written thank-you notes are powerful tools that greatly increase the number of referrals a salesperson receives. The following personal experience will illustrate this statement. When new in the business, I did what managers tell all new salespersons to do in an effort to find customers. I cold-called a list of people compiled from a reverse street directory. At this point in the book I know that you realize that there are much better ways to prospect than cold-calling. At the time it was all I knew how to do.

I was lucky enough to call a young man in the Air Force who was as inexperienced at being a homeowner as I was at being a real estate salesperson. We chatted for about 15 minutes about real estate in general. After the call I wrote him a thank-you note and included my business card but I was so naive and disorganized that I did not bother to keep his name.

I could not have made a more basic mistake. As a member of the Air Force, this fellow was almost sure to be transferred in the next two to three years. He was a perfect Future File prospect. However, I was so busy trying to make a living I was not worried about two years down the road. I did not even have a permanent customer file, let alone an organized Future File.

Somehow I lasted in the business. Eighteen months later I received a call from my young Air Force man, who said: "Hi, Jim, this is Dave Prospect. I've received orders and will be leaving in about three months. Can you come out and tell me what my house is worth?"

"Sure," I said, "I'm looking forward to working with you."
We made an appointment. I drove to the house immediately
after the call. The first thing I saw upon entering was my thank-
you note sitting on a pile of papers stacked on his living-room
coffee table. After an exchange of pleasantries, he casually
stated, "When I found out I was being transferred, I dug out
my packet of real estate papers. I had put your note with them
when I received it. When I saw your note, I remembered your
call and decided a person who thought enough of me to send
this note deserved my business."

Whether I deserved his business is debatable. But I did get
it and I got it only because I had written a simple thank-you
note. I listed his house and sold it myself in three weeks. I would
not have gotten his business had I not written that thank-you
note and included a business card. His was the first of many
personal notes I have written since that day. This one experience also provided the nudge I needed to get organized, start a
customer file, and initiate a newsletter program. I hope reading
about this gives you the boost you need to do the same.

You can write a note of appreciation in a few minutes. It
need not be long or fancy. Other than saying "thanks," it is not
what you say that counts. The fact that you took the time and
cared enough to write a personal note to someone who did not
expect it makes it effective.

TOMBSTONE FILES

This exceptionally good approach for new salespersons requires
your sales manager's approval and assistance. In some locales,
these files are considered confidential by managers, precluding
the use of this approach. It consists of "adopting" former
customers of salespersons no longer with your company. Start
by compiling a list of all sales in previous years in which a
salesperson from your company was the selling salesperson.
Eliminate all people who bought their houses from salespersons
still with your company. This will pare the list down to sales
made by salespersons no longer affiliated with your firm. The
salespeople may be affiliated with other real estate companies
or no longer in the business.

The homeowners on this list provide new salespersons
with lists of prospective customers. Contact the owners indi-

vidually using a combination telephone/personal visit/follow-up letter approach. When calling, introduce yourself and state your company affiliation. Explain that your company is updating its files on all homeowners who purchased their houses through your agency. Tell them that the manager has assigned you to update their file, as the salesperson who sold them the house is no longer with your company. Initiate a discussion about the house and how it is serving the owner's needs. Let them know in a positive way that both you and the agency you are affiliated with are interested in the welfare of all previous customers.

After you have established yourself on the phone, arrange an appointment to visit them at their home if possible. This gives you and the homeowners a chance to become acquainted. Let the owners show off their house, kids, and hobbies. Answer any questions they have about real estate. If they request information that requires research, make a note of it. It is also acceptable to ask for referrals at this time. Immediately after meeting the owners in person, send a thank-you note or letter. If the owners requested information you did not have or had questions you could not answer when you met them, get back to them as soon as possible.

Add these homeowners to your personal customer file. Mail them a recent issue of your newsletter and place them on the newsletter mailing list. These "orphaned" homeowners provide a golden opportunity for hungry salespersons. In very little time you will have developed a list of 50 potential customers. Researching the closed-sales file is another activity in which you can profitably use otherwise unproductive time.

PERSONAL PROSPECTING

Personal prospecting consists of prospecting for sellers in your daily encounters with the public. You can significantly increase your permanent customer list at no cost and with a minimum of effort by regularly seeking business from the people you meet every day. Candidates for personal prospecting generally fall into four categories:

1. New acquaintances,
2. People with whom you do business,

3. Neighbors, and
4. Friends.

We will look at each of these individually.

New Acquaintances

When meeting people for the first time, you need to let them know you sell real estate for a living if you are to find out if they are or know potential business prospects. However, this should not be the basis upon which to build your initial conversation. The correct approach when meeting someone for the first time is to develop the conversation around the other person's interests. Center the conversation on his or her family, profession, or hobbies. When you show interest in another person, that person will think highly of you.

After a time the conversation in most cases shifts to you and what you do for a living. This is the time to introduce the subject of real estate. Answer any questions the other person has and pursue any leads the conversation produces. Use your best judgment as to when you should drop the subject of real estate. Do not create the impression that the only reason you are talking to the person is to obtain real estate leads.

When wrapping up the subject of real estate, ask your new acquaintances for their permission to add them to your newsletter mailing list. Let them know that they do not need to be thinking of buying or selling to receive the newsletter and that there is no cost or obligation involved. Occasionally they will protest that you will be wasting your time and money. Explain that your newsletter program is a service that you provide for everyone you know and that most people that receive it find it informative and useful even if they are not planning on conducting any real estate business. In most cases they will allow you to add them to your mailing list and your permanent customer file.

People with Whom You Do Business

All people you give business to are included in this category. Compile this prospect list by going through your checkbook stubs and charge card statements. Any person or business you buy goods or services from should be on this list. The only exceptions are out-of-town businesses or large corporations where you rarely deal with the same person twice.

Include all people with whom you do business on a cash basis. This group could include gas station owners or attendants, grocery store owners or check-out clerks, fast-food restaurant owners, newsstand operators, and any other merchant with whom you deal regularly. Do not forget businesses with which you use a bank or department store charge card. Update your list often to keep it as comprehensive as possible. Obtaining referrals from this group requires a consistent effort. Talking real estate every time you see them is a big plus in obtaining the maximum number of referrals possible. Benefit from the fact that people love to talk business, yours and theirs.

Discuss trends in interest rates, sales volume, new home-building activity, or any other real estate topic the person is interested in. Follow up by asking about possible real estate leads of which they may be aware. Make it a point to specifically ask if they know of any selling or buying prospects. If you neglect asking, you will miss the majority of the leads available from this source.

People in this group of prospects are like you in that they are prospecting for business on a regular basis. They are not offended by prospecting inquiries. They expect them. By asking for referrals on a regular basis, you remind them that you want not only their business but every prospect lead they can give you. Earn these referrals by asking for them and then providing superior service. Like all of your customers, these people belong on your permanent customer list and your newsletter mailing list. They should receive all the benefits of being one of your customers.

Neighbors

Turn your neighbors into customers by becoming the neighborhood real estate expert. Take every opportunity to inform them of changes in the local real estate market that will have an effect on your neighborhood and real estate values in general. Tell them about new subdivisions, planned shopping centers and those under construction, changes in the local tax structure, or any other event that will affect the local marketplace. Become the source for what is happening in real estate in your neighborhood. Join your neighborhood association. Be the secretary/treasurer if possible so that you can sign the neighborhood newsletter. Be available to help with real estate problems or questions. Do not hesitate to ask for leads. Look at the person across the back fence as a potential source of business.

Friends

It is poor form to seek leads from your friends. Friends will provide you with leads because they are your friends. And when they do, you should follow some common-sense practices. Treat every prospect they refer to you as a special person deserving of extraordinary service. Treat them as the most important referrals you will ever receive. They are, because your friends have put their reputations as well as yours on the line.

SOURCES FOR YOUR CUSTOMER FILE

When compiling your personal customer list, add every person in all of the following groups of people that you know on a personal basis or who would have reason to know who you are.

- Every person you know who owns any type of real estate
- Everyone with whom you do business
- All social acquaintances
- Fellow church members
- Relatives by blood or by marriage
- People you have worked with in previous jobs
- Former schoolmates (use your yearbooks as a source)
- Customers generated from prospecting
- Your doctor, dentist, attorney, and insurance agent
- Your paper carrier (chances are, his or her parents own a house)
- Neighbors
- Your spouse's workmates
- Fellow PTA members
- People on your Christmas card mailing list
- Your mail carrier
- Fellow civic club members
- Sports cronies: golf, tennis, bowling
- Parents of your children's friends

Every adult or near adult who knows you well enough to say "hi" when he or she sees you should be on this list. Most people know between 200 and 300 people on a first-name basis. As an established real estate salespersons, you will know many more. After being in business for three or more years, you should have a minimum of 500 to 600 families or individuals on your list. After three years over half of your business should result from referrals received from this group. Build your referral business by continually expanding your file. Include every person you can think of. Update and maintain this file in a businesslike manner. The benefits are enormous.

By consistently building and maintaining a personal customer file, you can increase your listing and sales volume throughout your career while reducing prospecting time. Keeping in contact with these people is the most effective way to increase the number and quality of referrals. The most time-effective method of staying in contact is through the consistent application of a newletter program. The greatest positive impact you can make with past, present, or prospective customers is by providing service when people least expect it. Build and maintain your client file as outlined in this chapter, and the referrals will roll in.

EPILOGUE

The techniques explained in this book work. Apply them. They will work for you and you will prosper.

INDEX